Boomers on the Loose®

Boomers on the Loose®

Staying Healthy, Active, and Engaged in Retirement

Janet Farr

Boomers on the Loose® LLC
Olympia, Washington

IBSN: 978-0-9989871-2-5

Library of Congress Control Number: 2022920052

VOLUNTEERS
ANIMAL LOVERS
OUTDOORSIES
CULTURE BUFFS
ARTSY CREATIVES
HOBBYISTS
READERS, WRITERS
LEARNERS, TEACHERS
FITNESS EXERCISERS
MUSIC NUTS
HISTORY ENTHUSIASTS
BUSINESS ENCORES

Table of Contents

Do More Of It

Seems a lot of people, spend a lot of time
Trying to get happy, and finding peace of mind
To me it's very simple, to live your life and love it
Just find what you like to do, and do more of it

To some it's driving fast in a car
To some it's flying high with the stars
To some it's traveling near and far
To some it's staying right where they are

Some like dancing all night long
Some like singing and playing a song
Some folks live as if it's a race
While others like a slower pace
Doesn't really matter, what puts a smile on your face

All I'm really trying to say
You want to have a better day?
Just find what you like to do, and do more of it
Yes, it's really very simple, to live your life and love it
Just find what you like to do, and do more of it

Tim Flumerfelt, Musician, Songwriter
1954 - 2022

INTRODUCTION

It's a great time to be a Baby Boomer.

Every day, Boomers are discovering that "retirement" is simply an avenue toward "re-inventment!" Life isn't winding down for Boomers – it's amping up! And that's why this book is chock full of exciting retirement ideas and choices – to make it easy for you to find exactly what you want to do and be in this exciting new life chapter.

Boomers on the Loose® is a light-hearted reference guide to hundreds of activities and leisure options for retiring or retired Baby Boomers and others who want their post-career years to be active and meaningful. (An expanded set of questions is available for download at boomersontheloose.com)

Research shows that Boomers want to live with purpose and fulfillment. They want to be active and productive. They want to dig in the dirt, plant, and harvest community gardens, and restore wetlands and wildlife habitat. They like to guide groups around nature centers, art galleries, and museums. Shelve library books. Serve on public committees. Teach kids to read, play music, dance, garden or create art. Learn music, lead hikes, paddle dragon boats, walk goats at the zoo, count birds, and clean up parks. Retirees learn new skills and start new careers and businesses. They study the world, meet new people, volunteer, improve our communities, travel, and lots more.

As I first heard Tim strum and sing "Do More of It" – it struck me – his lyrics were a simple, clear expression of my book's purpose and example of someone who, through his music, lives it.

"To live your life and love it, just find what you like to do and do more of it."

Boomers on the Loose® will help you with the "find" part, the "do" part is up to you.

Jan Farr, Author

We hope you're getting the idea that Boomer status can be pretty darn exciting!

We also realize that retirement can be intimidating – "What do I do now?" That's exactly why created *Boomers on the Loose®* was created – to guide you on your quest for "what's next?" In this book, you'll learn more about how and where to pursue your existing and hidden interests or develop new ones.

Staying Healthy, Active, and Engaged

More and more research (and often our own experience!) is uncovering the habits, activities, and lifestyle choices that greatly enhance and enrich our retirement experience. As you consider the abundance of choices available to you, also consider weaving these life-enriching practices into this next life chapter.

- **Maintaining physical health.** When we're healthy, we optimize what is possible for us. To live our best retirement lives, we need to make good lifestyle choices about exercise, sleep and eating. Good choices help us live longer, happier lives.

- **Boosting brain health.** Physical and mental health are closely related. Activities that deliver more oxygen to the brain can boost brain health. Among a long list of brain-nourishing activities are exercise, learning, being outside, volunteering, and social activities.

- **Learning new things.** Our lives become richer when we immerse in a hobby, attend or teach classes, learn more about ourselves, our world, and communities, or delve into something creative such as crafts, art, performance, photography, or music.

- **Giving back.** Your time and energy make the world a better place through volunteering and community service. Volunteering enriches our lives with the satisfaction of helping others.

- **Engaging socially.** We are hard-wired social creatures. Our interactions with family and friends create positive feelings of wellbeing. Closely related and equally as important, we innately need to belong and feel valued in our communities.

- **Appreciating your world**. Enjoy the accomplishments of mankind, including your own. We find meaning in the advances of knowledge and expression of humanity in all forms. We explore that by traveling, reading, and engaging in cultural activities.

- **Getting outside.** Being outdoors is good for us and we are blessed with abundant opportunities to experience nature's wonders. Make it a priority to visit, appreciate, and respect the natural features and areas in your own communities.

- **Taking time to be still**. Express gratitude every day. Put aside mind-clutter and to-dos and focus on just being silent. Be grateful for the abundant blessings and opportunities we enjoy in life.

So now get ready to do something big, Boomers.

Dive in and use *Boomers on the Loose®* as an all-in-one-place tool to zero in on and experience your passions.

How *Boomers on the Loose®* is Organized

As a way of organizing an ever-expanding number and wide variety of retiree options, *Boomers on the Loose®* is organized into two parts:

Self-Understanding Section. *CHAPTER 1: WHO AM I?* offers a series of questions to help you think about your vision of retirement, values, passions, personality, skills, experience, and other "you traits" that influence what you want to do and express in retirement.

Interest Area Section. CHAPTERS 2-27. "Interest area" in this book refers to broader categories of activities, for example, volunteering, arts, music, animals, outdoors, learning, etc. *CHAPTER 2: INTEREST AREAS* summarizes the interest area categories described in greater detail in CHAPTERS 3-27. In these chapters, you'll learn more about activities and options that may naturally appeal to you.

The chapters offer a handy jump-off point for researching your areas of interest in your own community.

Note about the interest area of Volunteering: *Because volunteering and giving back is such an important focus for many retirees, volunteering activities are not only the focus of CHAPTER 4: VOLUNTEERING but are described in many other interest area chapters throughout the book.*

How to Use This Book

You can approach this book and its core interest area descriptions either separately or together and dig into as much detail as you need. Our guide details activities organized by popular interest areas.

For the best results, we recommend that you:

1. In *CHAPTER 1: WHO AM I?* complete the "Who Am I" questions. Your responses will help you be aware of your bigger vision and what you uniquely bring to this life chapter – the values that you live, your favorite natural and acquired abilities and skills, your passions, and general areas of interest. Once you've thought about the package that is you, it's time to think about specific types of interests that attract you.

2. In *CHAPTER 2: INTEREST AREAS*, identify your area(s) of interest – broader categories of popular retiree interests – from the summaries provided. Look through summaries for categories that speak to you in some way. From there, you can begin to zero in on specific organizations and options that you may find appealing.

3. For the interest areas you select, visit the corresponding interest area chapter(s), CHAPTERS 3 - 27, for more detail including other questions to consider. Topics are further divided into other layers of interests, introducing ideas and options for enthusiasts.

4. Once into your interest area, dive deeper by learning even more or getting involved in the activity. Search online for local organizations or situations by your interest and visit their websites. Begin with the name of your community (city, state) and type of organization. Visit their pages or contact them for more detail.

5. Create an informal or detailed action plan using the "Action Plan" template provided below:

   - Define your specific area of interest. For example, hiking and walking, community service or volunteering, etc.

   - Specify the organization and/or type of activity of interest. For example, libraries, helping kids learn to read; swing dancing, boating, learning music, studying history, starting a business.

   - Make notes and write down your questions about what more you need to know about an activity or organization by doing our own research.

   - Identify the next steps to take to decide if it might be a good opportunity for you. For example, search online for information about related activities and organizations, attend a meeting, contact an organization directly.

- Put specific action steps on your calendar. For example, join a meetup group, visit websites, research elsewhere, talk with a specific organization or talk with people involved in the activity, contact a group or club leader.

- In the Action Plan Worksheet, write in reference information such as contact name, phone number, email address, and questions, and notes regarding next steps.

- If you believe this might be a good fit, try out the activity.

Action Plan Worksheet

Use these headings to create your own worksheet on separate sheets of paper.

Area of Interest	Specific Activity or Organization	What More Do I Need to Know?	Action / Next Steps

A Clear Journey
LOST IN THE '90S
ANIMALS
TAKE ACTION
DO MORE OF WHAT YOU LOVE

CHAPTER 1: WHO AM I?

Transitions in our lives are a good time to go back to basics and think about what makes you, you. A clearer understanding of yourself and your retirement aspirations will help you zero in on the activities that appeal to you and where to go from here.

The following questions will help you be aware of your bigger vision and what you bring to this life chapter—the values that you live, your favorite natural and acquired abilities and skills, your passions, your general areas of interest. Think carefully about your responses, completing the sentence prompts with how they relate to you.

If you would like to explore these question prompts in greater detail, download the *About Me* questions, exercises, examples, and other self-understanding tools at boomersontheloose.com.

What Is My Vision?

Your vision is your mental picture of your in this next phase of your life. What does the future feel and look like to you? What do you want to see, experience, create, learn, and accomplish? Who do you want to experience life with? Probably even more important, what should retirement feel like?

In retirement, I see myself… (what types of activities do you imagine yourself doing in retirement?)

For me, retirement should feel like… (include words that show how you want to feel in retirement, for example, happy, fulfilled, energetic, thoughtful, relaxed, etc.).

What Am I Passionate About?

Passions are experiences you get so immersed in that you lose track and sense of time and place. Passions are a major influence on choices we make in our lives. We may be passionate about the relationships in our lives, a cause, an activity, or a place. Our passion may be interacting in some way with animals, being outdoors, cooking, traveling, or a combination. Knowing our passions adds another piece of the "me" puzzle. Living our passions makes us smile.

The experiences in life that make me smile are… (describe the people, activities, and other experiences that truly bring joy and meaning to your life).

Activities that I enjoy so much that I totally lose track of time are…

What Values Do I Live By?

Our personal values are concepts, traits, or beliefs that guide the ways we live and work. What we value influences nearly everything we do – our lifestyle, decisions, behaviors, choices, and emotions. Examples of values are health, commitment, fairness, family-oriented, and honesty.

The values that guide my everyday life decisions and activities are… (describe the values that are reflected in how you live your life).

To help you examine the values that guide your life, download the *My Values* worksheet at boomersontheloose.com.

What is My Personality Like?

Each of us is made up of unique set of personality traits that come into play when we consider "what's next?" We are drawn to activities that line up with our personalities, as well as other preferences. Some people, for example are highly social; others prefer solitude. Some want physical activity; others enjoy mental challenges.

The words I would use to describe my personality are … (describe a few of your dominant personality traits).

To help you define your dominant personality traits, download the *My Personality* worksheet at boomersontheloose.com.

What Do I Do Well?

One goal of many retirees is to make the best use of what they do or know well – the skills, abilities, knowledge, and unique experiences acquired through work, volunteering, hobbies, and just doing life. For many, using our skills and knowledge in purposeful, meaningful ways enhances our retirement experience.

I am the most proud of my abilities to... (describe what you believe are your best skills and abilities, for example organizing, communicating, building something, cooking, sewing, managing, acting, playing an instrument, etc.).

The skills and abilities I'd most like to use in retirement are ...

To help you examine the values that guide your life, download the *My Skills* worksheet at boomersontheloose.com.

What Life Lessons Do I Want to Apply?

At this time in our lives, we can usually point to specific life experiences that have impacted our lives and provided insight into ourselves, our priorities, and what we value. Examples are often found in personal academic, career, or sports accomplishments, experiencing a serious illness, the births and deaths of loved ones, experiences involving college, travel, classes, books, and many others.

The life experiences that taught me the most were... (describe the most life changing experiences or events during your life).

The most important lessons I learned from these experiences were...

To help you explore and define important life experiences, download the *Life Lessons Learned* worksheet at boomersontheloose.com.

What are My Gifts to the World?

Each of us brings an individual package of values, skills, experience, expertise, passions, and interests with a unique-to-us view to the world. That package changes as we grow, mature, and experience transitions in our lives. Wrapping those within your vision, you'll discover a picture of what you uniquely offer in this world. Large or small, our gift is uniquely ours. Many of us find meaning and purpose expressing that which only we can offer.

What makes me different and unique is… (describe what you uniquely bring into your world of retirement).

To help you discover and define the unique gift you offer, download the *My Unique Gifts* worksheet at boomersontheloose.com.

What Other Questions Should I Consider?

Other questions you might think about in this process include:

- *What have I always wanted to try? Is it time to go in a totally new direction?* Now might be that time to pay attention to a desire to learn renew a new or back-burner activity. For example, you've been a corporate accountant but always wanted to teach. *Is it time to switch careers to teaching or do something totally different?*

- *What are my family commitments? What family commitments do I need to work with or around? Or should I spend more time with family and friends?*

- *What financial considerations do I have? What can I afford? Many pursuits are free or low cost. Is the availability or cost of transportation or other factors a consideration?*

- *What other limitations should I consider, such as health or physical conditions, location, or other obligations such as caregiving?*

CHAPTER 2: INTEREST AREAS

Our interests, along with activities that attract us, are influenced by our vision, values, skills, and personality, and often, our upbringing and many other things. Now that you've considered the package that is you, it's time to narrow your search and see what interests attract you.

Below you'll find summaries of popular interest areas (categories of activities) which make up the core chapters of this book. Looking at the summaries, you can begin to apply the self-understanding you acquired by working through *CHAPTER 1: WHO AM I?*

For the interest areas that speak to you, look for the corresponding interest area chapter. Within each chapter, you find a more in-depth description of activities and opportunities within that category.

Then you can go a step further and begin your own research on specific options in your own community that may appeal to you.

Popular Interest Areas

The following are summaries of the interest categories under which popular retiree activities are grouped and detailed in Chapters 3-27.

Animals. Find your niche in organizations that rescue and care for dogs, cats and other small animals, horses, birds, and other animals.

Help take care of animals at rescue organizations. Or get your pet certified as a therapy animal for friendly visits at places such as nursing homes and care facilities. See *CHAPTER 4: ANIMAL LOVERS* on page 39.

Art, Photography, Film. Engage in your favorite art form, expressing yourself through art, photography, or filmmaking…or other art form. Take classes, visit your favorite gallery, or volunteer as a docent, curator, teacher, or in a behind-the-scenes office or another role. See *CHAPTER 5: ART, PHOTOGRAPHY, FILM* on page 43.

Business Building. Turn a passion, interest, or hobby into a business. Examples are consulting, jewelry-making, writing, and blogging, on-line retail, professional services such as accounting and bookkeeping, and more. See *CHAPTER 6: BUSINESS BUILDING* on page 47.

Care for the Environment. Seek opportunities in environmental organizations, friends-of-parks, parks and recreation activities, and public gardens. Volunteers restore parks, natural and wildlife areas, plant trees, shrubs, and flowers, teach and guide groups, and advocate for environmental causes. *See CHAPTER 7: CARE FOR THE ENVIRONMENT* on page 51.

Career Encores. Explore options to stay in the workforce or ease into retirement such as continuing in another full or part-time role, changing careers or employers, seeking new training, or working for a nonprofit. See *CHAPTER 8: CAREER ENCORES* on page 55.

Community Service. Volunteers give back to help people who are disabled, hungry and homeless, or face health and mental health challenges with many nonprofit and faith-based organizations. Work in direct service, outreach activities, and administrative and technology areas. See *CHAPTER 9: COMMUNITY SERVICE* on page 57.

Events and Festivals. Retirement gives us more time to enjoy events and festivals around sports, food and beverage, cars, nature, books, history, music, special interests, and far more. Go beyond attending or performing, to volunteering for behind-the-scenes roles essential to make events enjoyable. See *CHAPTER 10: EVENTS, FESTIVALS* on page 59.

Fitness, Healthy Living. Options for staying fit and healthy in retirement are plentiful, from walking and hiking to skiing and water sports, golf, pickleball, swimming, or visiting the gym. To make the most of retirement, commit to healthy living. Pick out activities that make you smile and go for it. See *CHAPTER 11: FITNESS, HEALTHY LIVING* on page 63.

Gardening. Release your inner, or outer gardener by hands-on dirt digging in a garden such as your own, or by volunteering to help care for a public or demonstration garden. Enroll in classes, teach one, or join a garden club. Help maintain gardens in community facilities. See *CHAPTER 12: GARDENING* on page 73.

Government Service. Look into a wide variety of volunteering opportunities with local government agencies. Serve on advisory boards, commissions, and committees; help at parks and recreation outdoor activities, farmers markets, city events and festivals; assist with various social services, or in justice and legal, and law enforcement offices. See *CHAPTER 13: GOVERNMENT SERVICE* on page 77.

Healthcare Volunteering. Bring your healthcare experience or interest to a volunteer role in a hospital, community health, mental health, or hospice setting. Or work for health-related causes you are passionate about or naturally connect with. Help with office and administrative tasks, and community outreach programs and events. See *CHAPTER 14: HEALTHCARE VOLUNTEERING* on page 81.

Hiking, Walking. As the retiree exercises of choice, walking and hiking are easy and good for you. Take in the fresh air and natural scenery in nearby communities, parks, urban routes, trails, forests, mountains, rivers, and wetlands. Join up your friends, or a walking and hiking club, or walk in an event. See *CHAPTER 15: HIKING, WALKING* on page 85.

Hobbies. Move a long-time interest, or back burner hobby to the top of the list. What do you want to do more of, collect, make, collect, or play? To get started, seek out on-line classes or workshops. take or teach a class, visit a hobby store, or join a club. See *CHAPTER 16: HOBBIES* on page 89.

Learn Something New. Transform your curiosity into knowledge, understanding, and appreciation. Take advantage of abundant learning venues including libraries, community college programs and classes, museums, parks and recreation programs, community centers, community organizations, retiree living communities, on-line classes and forums, and many other learning places. See *CHAPTER 17: LEARN SOMETHING NEW* on page 91.

Literary Arts, Reading, Writing. Retirees fulfill their reading desire at local libraries, using the technology of online readers, and downloads.

And help others through volunteering. Many retiree authors find their audiences through self-publishing books. See *CHAPTER 18: LITERARY ARTS, READING, WRITING* on page 93.

Museums, History. Dig into your favorite aspects of history at a wide variety of museums and learning places nearly everywhere. They preserve histories of natural features, communities, industry, art, architecture, transportation and more. Volunteers help in maintaining museums and artifacts and in other administrative, marketing, and reaching roles. *See CHAPTER 19: MUSEUMS, HISTORY* on page 97.

Music. Many Boomers renew, revisit, or redirect their love of music as they attend concerts, perform in various venues, learn an instrument, improve abilities, or teach. As music volunteers, they teach for nonprofits, help with music events, and play music to help causes they care about in settings such as hospitals, hospice, and nursing homes. See *CHAPTER 20: MUSIC* on page 101.

Senior Assistance. Pay-it-forward volunteers give back by serving in nonprofits and other organizations that help seniors in daily living activities such as transportation, meals, learning and social activities, in-home assistance, grocery delivery and others. See CHAPTER 21: *SENIOR ASSISTANCE* on page 105.

Sharing Wisdom. Organizations specifically built upon the life skills and experience that senior adult volunteers offer in areas such as teaching, training, management, accounting, working with youth, and many others. See *CHAPTER 22: SHARING WISDOM* on page 107.

Social Connections. Innate to our humanity, we seek connection with others. We connect anywhere we gather around a common interest such as neighborhoods, faith organizations, hobby and interest groups, community centers, in volunteer activities, and many more places. See *CHAPTER 23: SOCIAL CONNECTIONS* on page 109.

Teaching, Speaking. Give back what you know to others through classes, workshops, and speaking in classrooms, libraries, and community centers or through service clubs, learning forums, and many other types of organizations. See *CHAPTER 24: TEACHING, SPEAKING* on page 111.

The Great Outdoors. Follow your passion for being outdoors by checking out opportunities, including volunteer activities, throughout several chapters of this book. Start your research with *CHAPTER 25: THE GREAT OUTDOORS* on page 117.

Theater and Performance. Retirees enjoy nearly unlimited ways to engage all varieties of theater experiences. Those who enjoy performing roles on or behind the stage can find community and regional theater companies to join a volunteer cast or take on any number of tasks to bring performances to life. See *CHAPTER 26: THEATER AND PERFORMANCE* on page 119.

Travel. If travel tops your bucket list, options for fun, once-in-lifetime trips are plentiful. Or stay closer to home and explore your own state, region, or community. See *CHAPTER 27: TRAVEL* on page 123.

Volunteering. For many Boomers, retirement is a time to use our time, experience, and skills to give back. It's no secret that giving back enriches our retirement experience. See *CHAPTER 4: VOLUNTEERING* on page 25.

As you work your way through the interest area chapters, you'll also notice that the activities described emphasize existing, mostly inexpensive, or free things to do or join in most communities.

This book suggests that you look at places like community colleges, parks and recreation programs, senior and community centers, community service and nonprofit organizations, government agencies, outdoor organizations, open-to-everyone clubs and groups, and your own living communities.

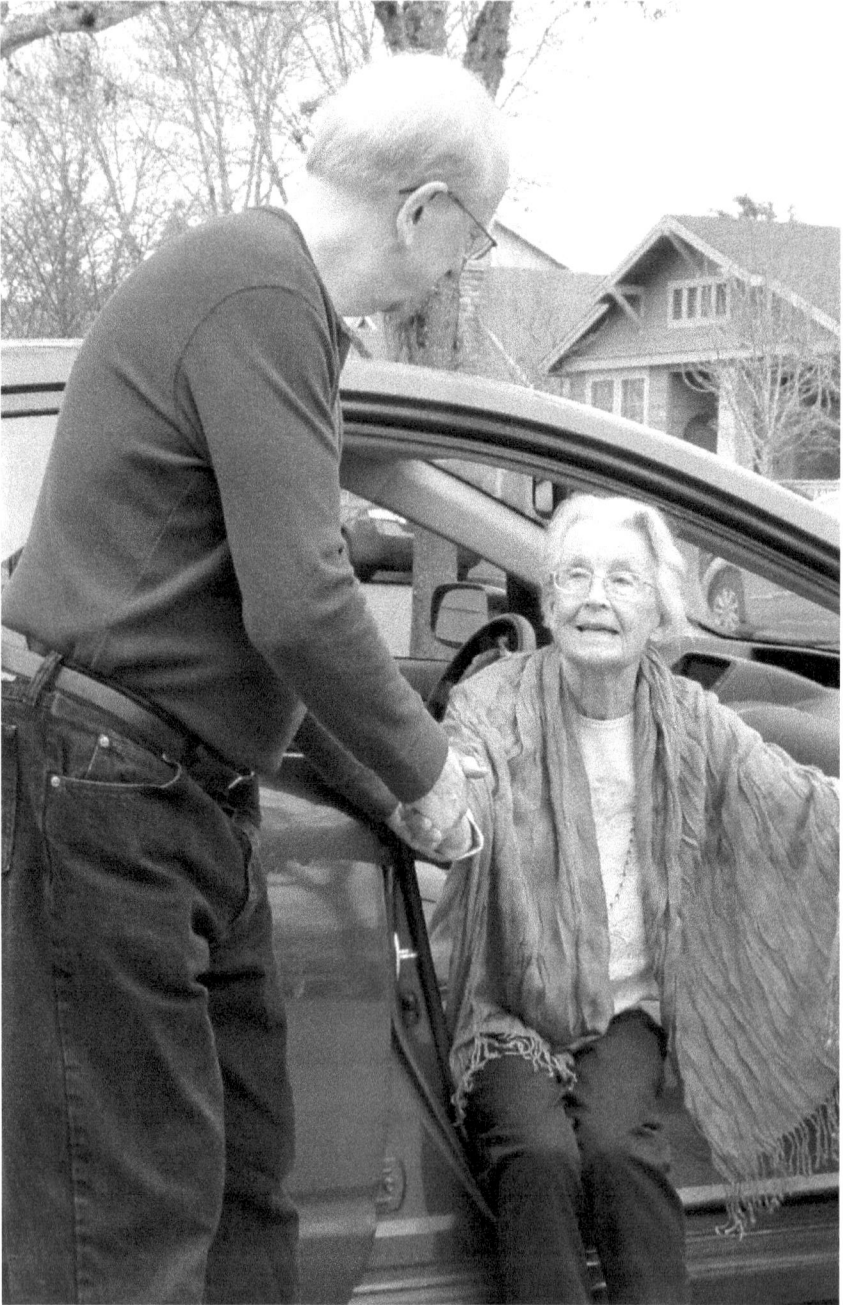

CHAPTER 3: VOLUNTEERING

Because so many retirees find meaning and purpose in giving back, the topic of volunteering appears here as a stand-alone chapter. Various types of volunteering activities are also described in several other interest areas chapters.

Where the categories are the same or similar between chapters, this chapter includes a short description of the activity, with references to more detail in other related interest area chapters.

The spirit of volunteerism among Boomer retirees reflects our love of life, our world, and each other. And for those of us in the active Boomer community, it's our time to give back to make our communities better places to live both now and in the future.

Retiring Boomers have more time on their hands and feel the need to give back. Instead of looking for being paid, Boomers now look to pay back in their communities.

Some people are drawn to a particular organization; others to a cause or issue that speaks to them. Many enjoy working with a specific age group such as kids or seniors. Handy retirees want to use their skills in new ways or learn a new skill. Some volunteers join with others to improve their neighborhoods and communities. Others find their callings within groups to which they already belong, such as faith communities or professional organizations, and quietly fill needs they see around them. Opportunities to give back are endless.

Why Retirees Volunteer

For many of us, retirement is a time to use our time, experience, and skills in a meaningful way. It's no secret that giving back enriches our retirement experience. Ask just a few of the millions of retiree volunteers across the county.

Volunteering, plain and simple, creates positive feelings and makes us feel better physically and mentally. Our brains are nourished when we feel purposeful, challenge ourselves, work in community, socialize, and, even most importantly, help others.

The feeling of making a difference gives us a stronger sense of purpose and fulfillment. The activity associated with volunteering enhances our health. We find greater meaning by using our time, energy, and unique gifts to improve the lives of others. For many, retirement is a time to share what we uniquely offer to serve others.

Think about it. What is your unique gift? What could you share that gives you meaning and joy?

At a time when we leave work and our social network all but disappears, volunteering opens us to new people and experiences. We naturally build new relationships, and learn new things, We broaden our social networks through connections with the people and communities we serve. Volunteering helps us enjoy a greater sense of camaraderie and community in sharing common causes and purposes.

It All Starts with You!

Confused about where to find a meaningful volunteer gig? Start with yourself, of course.

Finding the right opportunity means searching for organizations and situations that need what you can and want to do. You first need a good idea of your own reasons to volunteer, which include your preferred types of activity/service. Then you can look for the right organization or situation. Here's where to start:

1. Review your responses to questions in *CHAPTER 1: WHO AM I?* Your answers helped you clarify your values, passions, and general areas of interest. (You can also download the handout – *Discovering Your Ideal Volunteer Gig* from boomersontheloose.com for more self-understanding questions.)

2. Browse through the section below – *Popular Volunteer Paths* to see which may appeal to you or spark ideas for others. Many of the volunteer paths descriptions refer you to the related interest area chapters of this book for more information.

3. Next, find organizations with opportunities that match your skills, interests, and passions. These are as varied and diverse as the fabric of your community. Consider organizations that further causes you care about, the people they serve and how you can support them. Believe it, they want you!

4. If you're curious and adventurous, look into organizations you've never heard of, and just see what appeals to you. Sometimes friends can point you to an organization that you may want to look into.

5. Search for organization websites by your interest. Begin with the name of your community and type of organization. Visit their Volunteer pages or contact them directly for specifics.

6. Research the types of activities or organizations that match your interest through interest searches, then visit individual websites. Read their blogs and research news articles.

7. Check out the organization's vision, purpose, and mission. How does the organization carry out its purpose and serve its clients? Does it align with your values and personality?

8. Learn about the duties, responsibilities, and expectations of members or volunteers as well as the requirements and application process. Background checks of volunteers may be required.

9. See how website represents the organization; for example, does the website feel welcoming to new members, volunteers, and others? Is information, such as ways to contact. easy to find?

10. Set up an appointment with the volunteer coordinator and visit the organization to observe volunteers at work. Talk with other volunteers or members for their perspectives on the activity or volunteer opportunity.

11. Try out an activity, if possible, with other members or volunteers. How welcoming are they to new people?

Popular Volunteer Paths

Below are summaries of interest areas that commonly attract Boomer volunteers. Look for a category that speaks to you and learn about the types of volunteers typically needed. Many of these volunteer paths are also described in more detail in the interest area Chapters 2-27. Those chapters are referenced within the descriptions below.

Animal Lovers

Retirees enjoy many options to make a positive difference in our world through our connections with animals. Get involved in any number of roles in small or large animal rescue, people-pet team therapy involving pets, horses, and other animals, and wildlife preservation. See *CHAPTER 4: ANIMAL LOVERS* on page 39.

Art, Photography, and Film

Behind-the-scenes volunteers in diverse art communities serve as docents and curators; they work in gift shops, sell concessions, or put teaching, writing, photography, website, and office skills to work in many types of organizations. They help design and build exhibits and perform other roles to use enhance the experience for others. See *CHAPTER 5: ART, PHOTOGRAPHY, FILM* on page 43.

Business, Career, and Professional Organizations

Your own professional organizations or unions represent opportunities to volunteer while staying current in your field. These organizations need volunteers from within the ranks to carry out projects and education programs for members and often the community at large. Business owners may associate with any number of organizations that need volunteers either in leadership or worker bee roles. Career and professional organizations help members with information and services that develop and advance their skills.

Community Service

Volunteers give back in direct service or behind-the-scenes roles to help the disabled, hungry, homeless, and people facing health and mental health challenges at many faith-based organizations and nonprofits. See *CHAPTER 9: COMMUNITY SERVICE* on page 57.

Community Service Clubs

These groups serve the community through programs and projects that benefit various groups. In addition to leadership roles, their projects typically are operated entirely by member volunteers. They address the needs of various ethnic, cultural, religious groups, and age groups, through a wide variety of community projects, meetings, and events. Examples are Kiwanis, Urban League, Junior League, Lions Clubs, community health centers, and many other types of organizations.

Many organizations help support a nonprofit or community organization through year-round projects? Could you pitch in to help with planning or special events, or use your ideas to organize one?

Current Connections

Organizations to which you belong may offer the easiest way to "dip your toe" in the water of volunteering. Consider taking on a volunteer role with organizations in which you are active or have some other connection with. Consider business and career organizations, neighborhood groups, faith-based organizations, recreational and hobby clubs, and various clubs in retirement communities. You can serve as an officer or part of a project planning group or committee or help with a special event or fundraising event or taking on an occasional as-needed worker bee assignment. See the sections in this chapter including *Business, Career, and Professional Organizations, Faith-Based Organizations, Homes Associations, Neighborhood Service, Recreational, Hobby, and Special Interest Clubs*, and *Retiree Living Communities* for more examples.

Events and Festivals

The events and festivals we love so much need many behind-the-scenes volunteers to make them enjoyable. Volunteers help out at every stage of planning, holding the event, cleanup, and follow-up. A fun way to give back. See *CHAPTER 10: EVENTS, FESTIVALS* on page 59.

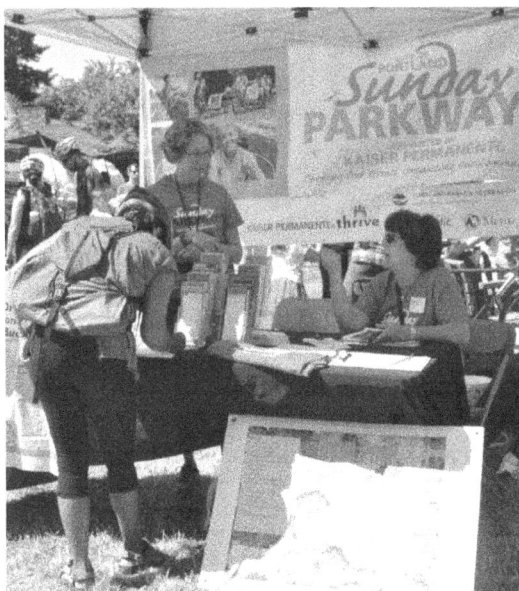

Faith-based Organizations

By nature, faith-based organizations offer compassionate help to one another and others in some way. Retiree volunteers benefit from a sense of connection to something beyond themselves, and benefit from social connections and the satisfaction of helping others.

Many provide support services for needy citizens, including the homeless, children, and others. There are numerous opportunities to give back and carry out your faith teachings.

How could you get involved with your faith community service projects and programs? For example, could you collect and sort clothes, prepare and serve food for homeless people, baby sit, or mentor youth?

Government Service

Surprising to many retirees are opportunities at local government agencies which include service on advisory boards, commissions, and committees; helping at parks and recreation outdoor activities, farmers markets, city events and festivals; assisting with various social services, city, or county-sponsored activities, and in justice and legal, and law enforcement offices. See *CHAPTER 13: GOVERNMENT SERVICE* on page 77.

Healthcare

Healthcare volunteers assist with patients in hospital, community health, mental health, and hospice settings. They work for health-related causes about which they are passionate or are naturally connected. They help with office and administrative tasks, and community outreach programs and events. See *CHAPTER 14: HEALTHCARE VOLUNTEERING* on page 81.

Home and Remote Volunteering

For whatever reason, Boomers want to volunteer, but can't physically leave home. So, what are some choices? With the widespread use of technology for communications and research, there are many options to explore. For example: AARP, RSVP (createthegood.aarp.org) program. Using the AARP website, you can search for opportunities for remote volunteer tasks which can be performed from home. At the volunteer-search page, enter the keywords "Volunteer from Home," and your zip code, and other criteria.

Other options for volunteering from home include:

- *Can you use the phone and computer?* If so, you may find organizations that need volunteers to make calls, send emails or do administrative work remotely.

- *Are you interested in writing notes, thank you notes, or invitations by hand?* Find organizations that need people to hand-write notes or address envelopes.

- *Could you write for an organization's newsletter or blog?* Could you write and submit a blog or article on something you know?

- *If you have a skill such as knitting or sewing,* could you help make blankets, quilts, scarves, or hats for the needy?

- *Will organizations bring work to you?* Perhaps for assembling baskets, stuffing envelopes. Or putting together flower arrangements.

- *Consider starting your own organization* to collect, package, and mail items, or create cards for men and women serving overseas. Put together backpacks of items for foster children.

Homes Associations

The boards and committees of Homeowners Associations carry out the bylaws of neighborhood communities and make decisions regarding maintenance of properties. Serving on a board gives you a direct say in issues affecting quality of life, home values, safety, and security. If you're new to a neighborhood, HOAs are good place to meet your neighbors and become more involved in your community. Boards welcome people of all backgrounds who bring plain skills, experience, and just plain good common sense to various roles.

What opportunities are available in your HOA? Could you put a special skill to work on your board, such as finance, or taking minutes, or working on the landscape committee. Or how about welcoming new residents? Or would you be better suited to one-time worker bee projects?

Libraries

City and county libraries need volunteers throughout library operations. They assist in computer labs, help with events, shelve books, check in materials, assist patrons, perform office and administrative tasks, teach classes, work with books, help in kids programs, and arts and crafts classes. "Friends" groups support their libraries. See *CHAPTER 17: LEARN SOMETHING NEW* on page 91 and *CHAPTER 18: LITERARY ARTS, READING, WRITING* on page 93.

Neighborhood Service

Boomers find and create fulfilling opportunities where they live. They get involved in both formal and informal groups of neighbors to support a project or a cause that benefits their community. They find a need and fill it, either individually or by joining together with others.

A good example is serving on, or starting, an emergency preparedness team. These teams help communities and individuals prepare for adversities ranging from power outages to chemical spills, to natural occurrences such as earthquakes, hurricanes, tornadoes, and floods.

Other volunteer opportunities within neighborhoods include maintaining community gardens and parks and creating informal groups to pursue common hobbies such as reading, sewing, woodworking, tennis, pickleball, or walking.

Without realizing it, many Boomers volunteer for caring activities in their neighborhoods by filling needs that arise in the community. For example, Boomers often watch out for and help their elderly neighbors with outdoor and pet tasks, grocery shopping, transportation, and little household chores, and provide a friendly visit to combat loneliness.

Are there needs in your own neighborhood that would improve security, or create a more inclusive, friendly community? Could you help with chores or run errands for someone having health or mobility problems?

Or provide a regular friendly visit or call to people who are homebound and isolated?

Nonprofits

The broad and large category of "Nonprofits" refers to organizations that exist for a social benefit (not to make a profit) and are defined as nonprofit for tax purposes.

Types of nonprofits include community service organizations, arts and cultural organizations, schools, churches, charities, homes associations, business associations, and social clubs; many of the types of organizations described elsewhere in this book.

Nonprofit organizations are an abundant source of opportunities to use your commitment, skills, and experience to give back. Nonprofits come in all shapes and sizes, with wide-ranging volunteering needs.

At the heart of all nonprofit organizations are committed volunteers who bring a wide variety of skills, interests, and talents to serve their communities and keep their organizations running. Whatever your skills and interests, you'll find a nonprofit eager to sign you up!

Especially welcome are volunteers with experience in business operations, or knowledge in the organization's area of focus or particular type of business. For example: healthcare, retail, marketing, or managing a nonprofit.

Volunteer tasks typically needed by nonprofits involve day-to-day operations, office and administration, marketing, technology support, and outreach. In many cases, nonprofits need lots of "arms and legs" volunteers ready to do whatever is needed to support their purpose. Volunteers get involved in working directly with an organization's clients or servicing them in some way. Assignments may be one-time projects, or ongoing daily, weekly, monthly, or seasonal. Volunteers also serve on governing boards and committees.

Museums and Historical Sites

A wide variety of museums preserve histories of communities and states, industry, art, architecture, transportation, home life, military, and more. Volunteers help preserve history and help others appreciate the past. You can work with a particular facet of history or focus on the history of your community. Opportunities are endless. See *CHAPTER 18: MUSEUMS, HISTORY* on page 97.

Music

Many Boomers express their love of music as volunteer teachers and performers in nonprofits that help people learn and enjoy music. They also perform to help causes they care about and in settings such as hospitals, hospice care, and nursing homes. Music festival volunteering is another option. See *CHAPTER 19: MUSIC* on page 101.

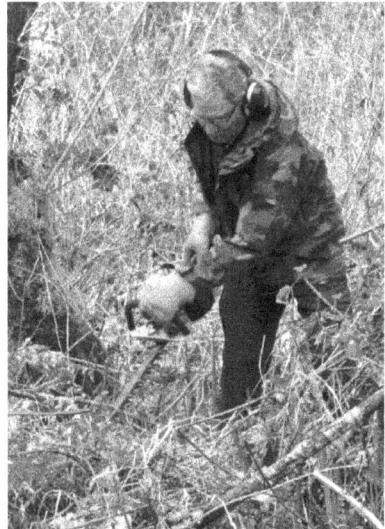

Outdoor Volunteers

Opportunities for outdoorsy types are plentiful in environmental organizations, friends-of-parks, parks and recreation activities and public gardens. Volunteers help restore parks, tend natural and wildlife areas, plant trees, shrubs, and flowers, as well as teach and guide groups, and serve as advocates for environmental causes. See *CHAPTER 7: CARE FOR THE ENVIRONMENT* on page 51 and *CHAPTER 25: THE GREAT OUTDOORS* on page 117.

Recreational, Hobby, and Special Interest Clubs

No matter what your interest or hobby, there is a club for it. Whether it be sports, DIY, arts, crafts, music, parenting, writing, or nearly anything, clubs are a great way to learn more and enjoy the ideas of like-minded people. And volunteers, of course, always are needed for any number of tasks, depending on the interest. Think about groups to which you belong and be aware of what you could offer. See *CHAPTER 16: HOBBIES* on page 89.

Retiree Living Communities

As retiree communities become more popular, residents volunteer within their communities to teach, organize, carry out special events, or informally volunteer to help others. You can find any number of one-time, seasonal, or ongoing ways to give back to the communities at large or serve on your community's board or committees.

Most communities always have open positions in areas such as communications, trips, education, entertainment, and social activities. You may also have an idea for a hobby or special interest group that would include volunteering. If so, start one.

How can you get more involved in your community's social activities and projects? For example, could you help with food, clothing, holiday gift drives? Could you adopt a nursing home or contribute time to a youth homeless shelter?

Senior Assistance

Many nonprofits, government agencies, faith-based and community service organizations sponsor programs to help seniors in daily living activities such as transportation, meals, learning, social activities, in-home assistance, grocery delivery, and many others. Organizations also help seniors with day-to-day needs. Retiree volunteers bring their own special connection and understanding to for the needs of these services and make great volunteers. See *CHAPTER 21: SENIOR ASSISTANCE* on page 105.

Sharing Wisdom

If you are a retiree who looks to apply the insight gained from life experiences, consider nonprofits and other organizations that tap into the experience of seniors to carry out their missions. These programs recognize the valuable contributions of older adults who make a difference in their communities. See *CHAPTER 21: SHARING WISDOM* on page 107.

Teaching and Speaking

What knowledge or expertise could pass along to others? Teach what you know through classes, workshops, and speaking in classrooms, libraries, and community centers or through service clubs, learning forums, and many other types of organizations. See *CHAPTER 24: TEACHING, SPEAKING* on page 111.

Theater and Performance

Theater lovers enjoy many opportunities to enhance the theater experience for themselves and others. Look for community and regional theater companies to join a volunteer cast or take on any

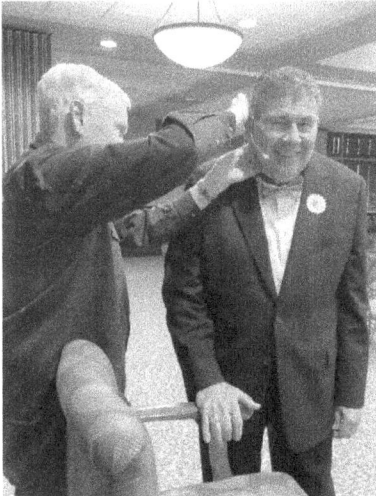

number of behind-the-scenes tasks to bring performances to life. See *CHAPTER 26: THEATER, PERFORMANCE* on page 119.

Unique and Informal Giving Back

Many people become naturally involved in volunteering using their unique interests and skills. Doing repairs, organizing youth baseball games, taking a disabled neighbor to lunch, playing music in a hospital waiting room, and checking with neighbors during an emergency.

Think again about the skills you've acquired in a past or current job or career. Are you good at building or fixing things, or figuring out technology? Calligraphy? Assembling something? Plumbing, carpentry, or electrical work? Car repair? Look for places that could use that skill, including many of those described elsewhere in this book. Some people turn their special interest into a Meetup group (meetup.com) to help others learn and participate in their interest.

So how do you find informal opportunities?

- Look around for needs that you could fill in your neighborhood or daily activities. Include your friends. *Who needs your help? Those who are elderly or disabled? New arrivals? Mothers with young children? Someone who experienced a serious health setback or lost a loved one?*

- Think about how to share your interests. *Pet lovers, could you walk dogs, or take your friendly pet to bring a smile to those in nursing homes?* (You'll need to get some training!) Or could you offer to help care for pets who reside with owners in assisted living facilities.

- Think about something you enjoy such as woodworking, jewelry making, or art, or some type of craft. *Could you donate your items to a nonprofit auction or gift store?*

- *If you knit, crochet, or sew, could you make blankets, hats, or scarves for needy adults and children?* Do some research. You'll come up with as many ideas as there are people with needs.

Volunteer Websites and Organizations

Another way to narrow your search for a volunteer opportunity is to visit websites of organizations that collect and post volunteer opportunities for many organizations. These include community-minded organizations such as chambers of commerce, and city and county websites. Some post job openings for their member businesses and organizations, and their nonprofit partners.

One popular site is VolunteerMatch.com which is used by nonprofits throughout the country to post volunteer opportunities. You can search for a gig that matches your location, interests, skills, and availability, and any other criteria you choose. For example, you can narrow it to one-time or ongoing projects, outside or inside, long-term, or short-term. Work with kids, adults, or seniors. In groups, or singly.

Below are examples of organizations that connect volunteers to multiple opportunities within their communities through their websites:

- AARP Real Possibilities. Helps seniors search for local volunteer opportunities. Search by keywords and zip code.

- Idealist. Connects volunteers to organizations with social impact.

- JustServe.org. A website where the volunteer needs of organizations may be posted and volunteers may search for places to serve in the community, providing opportunities to help those in need and enhance the quality of life in the community.

- United Way. Connects individuals, families, groups, and workplaces to volunteer opportunities such as tutoring, assistance in local disasters and emergencies, and more. Hundreds of nonprofits list ways to get involved as groups or individuals.

- VolunteerMatch. Volunteer website that helps volunteers connect with nonprofits, government agencies, and causes that need help.

More Thoughts on Volunteering

This process described above is intended as a starting point and path/process to lead you to meaningful volunteer work. Keep in mind:

- An important part of taking on a volunteer role is understanding your "why" – in other words, how you also will benefit. Take time to figure out your needs in the situation. Many who volunteer want to use their knowledge and skills in a meaningful way, learn new things, feel useful and appreciated, and make a difference. The social aspect of a common cause may also be extremely satisfying.

- Finding the right activities is an ongoing process. Much like a career, your ideas and interests change as you discover and pursue more options. While the basic you is still you, you may unexpectedly discover new ways to give back. As our world changes, so do the options available to you. Stay open.

- You may find what appears to be the "perfect" volunteer opportunity but then find that it just doesn't feel right. Remember, it needs to be a good fit. If intuition or common sense tells you otherwise, respectfully back away and move on, look at what you've learned, address it in a positive way and go forward.

- Much like nearly everything we try, there are new life lessons to learn. Expect to try a number of new things and enjoy it as part of life-long learning process.

CHAPTER 4: ANIMAL LOVERS

As humans, we share this planet – earth, water, air, and space – with other animals of every imaginable size, shape, and type. Many feel the calling to make the world a better place through love for, and connections with, other living creatures.

Animals we're closest to – our pets – give us a sense of purpose and meaning, motivate us to exercise, reduce isolation, give us a feel-good non-judgmental companion, and help us care for something outside ourselves.

If animals occupy your special heart place, get involved in animal-related volunteer work. You'll discover interesting, fulfilling and some out-of-the ordinary opportunities:

- Adopting and caring for our own pets.

- Volunteering at pet rescue and shelter organizations.

- Teaming up with a pet for joyful visits with adults and children confined to hospitals, nursing homes, and other care facilities.

- Working or volunteering with therapy animals such as cats, dogs, and horses to help people heal from physical and mental illness.

- Speaking out to advocate for animals in a variety of organizations.

- Caring for wild animals at zoos.

- Volunteering with organizations that preserve the quality of natural wildlife habitats.

Animal Adoption and Rescue

Every day, Boomers pour their love for animals into many channels of volunteer work to improve the lives of rescue cats, dogs, horses, birds, and other animals.

If your heart goes out to homeless, sick, abandoned, or abused animals, volunteering in animal rescue and adoption may be a rewarding activity for you. Many types of animal shelters are found in most communities and rely on volunteers to fulfill a wide variety of shelter caregiving jobs.

Small animal shelters always need volunteer help with animal feeding, socializing, fostering and adoption, transportation, and veterinarian care. Many also volunteer their time doing office and administrative work, or in outreach, marketing, and special events. Others offer their skills in photography, writing, graphic design, and technology.

Horse rescue operations care for at-risk horses that have been abandoned, abused, neglected, lost, or simply unwanted. They care for them until permanent homes can be found. Some operations combine horse rescue with equine-assisted therapy. See *Equine Assisted Therapy* below. Horse rescue involves similar tasks – feeding, grooming, cleaning stalls, fundraising, helping with special events, and doing clerical work, and other jobs.

Advocacy is another important function of animal rescue and adoption organizations. Animal advocates are the voices to protect animals in legislation and ordinances addressing animal treatment, speaking out and getting involved in causes to protect animals and prevent cruelty.

Animal Adoption and Rescue Organizations

To find places to adopt a pet or volunteer in a pet shelter, search for animal shelters in your community. Or visit any of these websites which allow you to search for available pets by city:

- Adopt a Pet. Nonprofit search site (adoptapet.com).

- Humane Society. National animal protection organization (humanesociety.org).

- Pet finder. Searchable database of animals who need homes (petfinder.com).

- Animal Shelter. Animal adoption website (animalshelter.org).

- Best Friends. National organization that saves lives of homeless pets (bestfriends.org).

To find places to work with shelter horses, search for equine or horse rescue in your community or visit these websites and search by city.

- Rescue Shelter. Provides links to horse rescue operations throughout the U.S. (horse.rescueshelter.com).

- Horse World Data. Provides links to horse rescue and retirement operations throughout the U.S. (horseworlddata.com).

Animal-assisted Therapy Programs

People-animal teams seek to improve the lives of others through friendly visits. They bring smiles to those they visit in hospitals, hospice care, nursing homes, mental institutions, treatment centers, and other places. Their visits calm the emotionally challenged, give confidence to the disabled, and connect to those with special needs.

Many libraries offer programs that help children improve reading skills by reading to special dogs, which by nature are, non-judgmental listeners.

Special training is often required to certify people-pet teams for animal-assisted therapy visits. Start with programs that offer training for animal-human teams such as:

- Love on a Leash. Animal therapy certification (loveonaleash.org).

- Pet Partners. Animal therapy certification (petpartners.org).

Equine-assisted Therapy Programs

If you enjoy working with horses and want to make a difference in lives of people, volunteer in an equine-assisted therapy program. Health professionals conduct animal-assisted programs as part of an individual's therapy. In equine-assisted therapy, for example, individuals receive hands-on training in horsemanship to address various disorders and disabilities. Search on-line for the websites of equine-assisted therapy programs in your area.

Wildlife Organizations

By participating in wildlife organizations, retirees contribute to the bigger picture of protecting our natural resources for the wellbeing of animals and humans alike. Options to get involved include volunteering, advocacy, fundraising, and activities at state and local levels. Check out the websites of wildlife organizations in your own community or national and international organizations such as:

- Audubon Society. Protects birds and their habitat (audubon.org).
- National Wildlife Federation. Protects and restores wildlife habitats (nwf.org).
- Conservation International. Conservation and nature protection (conservation.org).
- Jane Goodall Institute. Protection of chimpanzees and conservation of nature (janegoodall.org).
- National Resources Defense Fund. Focus on protecting plants, animals, and the natural systems (nrdc.org).
- Nature Conservancy. Preserves, protects natural resources (nature.org).
- Oceana. Focuses on protecting world's oceans (oceana.org)
- Sierra Club. Grassroots advocates for environmental protection (sierraclub.org).
- Wildlife Conservation Society. Global animal conservation program (wcs.org)
- World Wildlife Fund. Nature conservation and protection. (worldwildlife.org).
- 4Ocean. International organization works to clean oceans and coastlines and change plastic consumption habits (4ocean.com).

CHAPTER 5: ART, PHOTOGRAPHY, FILM

Does your interest gravitate to some aspect of visual art? If so, you'll discover a variety of places in your community to interact with your favorite art form by learning, teaching, volunteering, or participating in art-full communities of artists, photographers, and filmmakers.

Art is everywhere. You'll find collections and shows of every imaginable size and type of space and venue – public art galleries, museums, corporations, public and private buildings, spacious and tiny outdoor spaces, colleges, retirement communities – you name it.

Learn, Teach, Speak Art

If it's time to release your inner artist, no matter what your media, look for classes in museums, arts and cultural centers, community colleges, parks and recreation classes, community and senior centers and retirement communities. Other places to learn and practice art are visual arts, and film and photography clubs and organizations.

To enjoy your art through teaching or speaking, look for opportunities at the same places. For more ideas on where to learn or teach, see *CHAPTER 17: LEARN SOMETHING NEW* on page 91 and *CHAPTER 24: TEACHING, SPEAKING* on page 111.

Where Art Lives, Volunteers Follow

A variety of art-related volunteer opportunities are available to retirees. Boomers also express their art-loving sides in volunteer roles that range from working in a cultural center to helping youth learn about art, film, and photography. Most cultural nonprofits – regardless of size – rely heavily on volunteers to make exhibits, events, and programs available.

At larger galleries, many volunteer as docents – people who guide groups and help bring exhibits to life. Volunteers, including those with certain specialties perform a variety of other tasks such as working with artists, staff, and visitors, and setting up exhibits or writing blogs. Tasks may involve greeting visitors, assisting in a store or with office work, and helping at previews, receptions, fundraisers, and other events.

Festivals and events are another interesting option for artsy volunteers as they often need lots of volunteers for day and weekend shows.

Festivals offer a more relaxed atmosphere and volunteers may enjoy the benefits of free passes and refreshments, with some fun thrown in. Tasks include setup and take-down, ushering and hosting, and on-the-ground festival coordination and outreach. See *CHAPTER 10: EVENTS, FESTIVALS* on page 59.

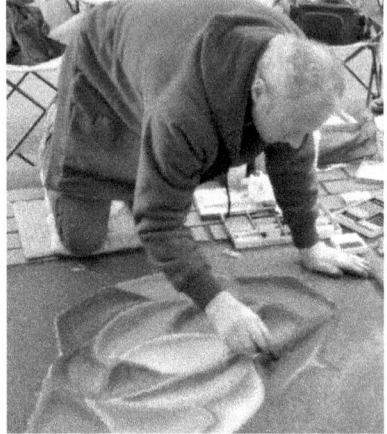

Youth Program Volunteers

Volunteering in youth art programs is another way to give back while expressing your artsy side. Volunteers help young people learn through classes, workshops, and special events. Find out more by researching places to teach youth art in your community such as family and youth nonprofits, schools, youth organizations, parks and recreation classes, arts and cultural centers, and after-school programs.

Art Commissions and Alliances

Art lovers like you help bring art to others by serving on various community, city, and county arts boards, committees, and commissions. These commissions invite and welcome participation in planning and overseeing community art projects.

By joining an art commission, you'll help promote the growth of arts and culture through public art projects, grants, advocacy, and special events, making art accessible to everyone. For more information, research the commissions and committees of your city, county, or regional planning entities.

Put Art and Graphic Skills to Use

You also can volunteer your artistic talents in graphic design, illustration, or desktop publishing for behind-the-scenes work with any number of organizations. Many need design and graphic arts skills in writing and photography, and creating websites, printed programs, brochures, posters, mailings, invitations, and more. To find graphic arts volunteer opportunities, research organizations in your interest area.

Photography, Film

Opportunities to practice, learn, teach, and volunteer in photography and filmmaking are similar to those enjoyed by other types of art enthusiasts. Photographers find learning and teaching opportunities in art and cultural centers, community colleges, community and senior centers, parks and recreation classes, and clubs, and Meetup groups.

The popularity of film and video media also has led to a growing number of college and university offerings in screenwriting and production.

Photography and Film Volunteers

Photographers with an interest in volunteering should look into stand-alone photo galleries, or galleries within art or historical venues. Opportunities may include serving as docents, maintaining collections, and helping at events and festivals, or in back-office roles.

Other options, whatever your skill, are community service and nonprofit organizations. For example, many animal shelters and rescue groups need photos for outreach and marketing activities. It's a great, fun way for amateurs to gain experience and add to a portfolio.

Other options for graphic arts volunteers include teaching in youth nonprofits, or other places such as community and senior centers, retirement communities, parks and recreation programs, and libraries.

Start your research for arts volunteers at individual nonprofit organizations in your interest area, libraries, or volunteering websites such as volunterMatch.com.

CHAPTER 6: BUSINESS BUILDING

Have you ever felt called to start and run your own business?

Some people find that turning their passions into businesses is the best way to express themselves and make their personal connections with the world. Their businesses are natural extensions of themselves and another way to live their passion or purpose.

Boomers who release their inner entrepreneur and go into business are in good company. We're aptly labeled Encore Entrepreneurs, and those who go it alone are called "Solopreneurs."

We're driven to run our own shows, challenged by turning our expertise and knowledge into a business. We create new uses for our experience – consulting or writing for example. We turn hobbies and passions into successful "lifestyle businesses." We offer products or services that we find meaningful and make a difference to others. Encores also embrace technology and the Internet to start and operate businesses. Add a touch of creative spirit, and Boomers find this an ideal time to go for their dreams.

Popular Business Options

While business opportunities are unlimited, examples of typical types of businesses Boomers engage in are:

- Consulting. Return to employers or an industry as consultants.

- Lifestyle. Turn an interest such as jewelry-making, crafts, woodworking, or collecting into a business.

- Writing and blogging. Share life experiences and expertise in a book or blog, or as a free-lance writer.

- Online. Establish an Internet or a website business to sell products, services, information, or some combination.

- Retail. Sell specialty products such as gifts, clothing and accessories, or food at a physical location.

- Public speaking, teaching, tutoring, or coaching. Inspire others and teach what you know in pursuits such as music, art, writing, sports, crafts, technology, and many others.

- Hang your shingle. Provide professional services such as writing, bookkeeping, accounting, marketing, or personal services.

Ask Yourself These Questions

Some questions you might ask yourself:

- What is my personal goal for having a business? Earn money, express myself in the world, follow a dream, etc.?

- What type of business do I want to start?

- What ability, skill, or interest could I turn into a business?

- How do I make my business unique and stand out from others?

- Who are my customers and how would my business benefit them?

Getting Started

Want-to-be entrepreneurs often don't know where to begin. Owning even a simple business has many pieces and parts to address, starting

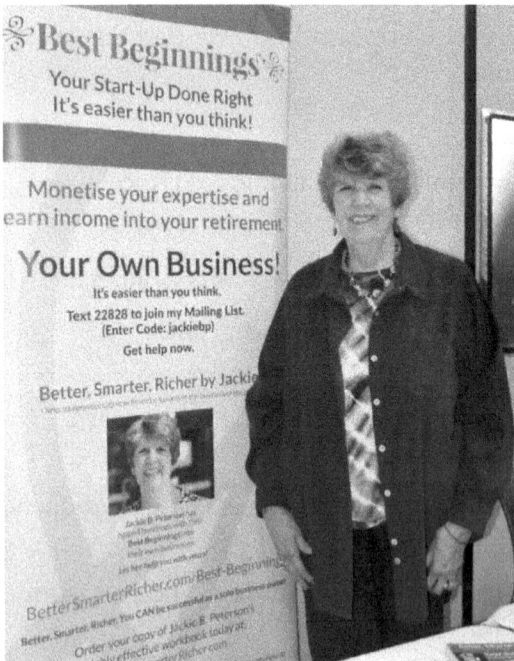

with decisions such as business name, form of business, state registration, and other legalities.

You need to determine specifics about your product or service, your customers and how to reach them, and how and where you will operate. Do you need employees? Physical equipment and supplies? What about office technology, a website, credit cards, bank accounts?

Not least among your decisions are how to finance and grow your business. All this leads to the necessity of a business plan. Fortunately, abundant help and resources are available to Encores no matter where you are with your business.

Small Business Development Centers

Small Business Development Centers provide counseling and training to small businesses including working with the Small Business Administration to develop and provide informational tools to support business start-ups and existing business expansion.

SBDCs throughout the country provide aspiring and current small business owners a variety of free business consulting and low-cost training services. Many local colleges and universities host regular SBDC activities. (sba.gov)

State Business Offices

The official state websites of most states provide easy-to-navigate information for businesses that operate within the state. Many detail steps on how to start a business and include practical and legal information about business names and structure, business plans, registrations, tax obligations, licenses, permits, and ongoing requirements.

Other Resources for Entrepreneurs

Other types of organizations with resources to help with launching and running a business include:

- SCORE. SBA-sponsored local chapters provide free mentoring and low-cost workshops. Working and retired executives and business owners donate time and expertise as business counselors. (score.org)

- Economic development organizations. As supporters of job creation, state and local economic development and chamber of commerce organizations provide access to resources and sponsor workshops for new business startups.

To learn more, research the websites of those types of organizations in your community.

CHAPTER 7: CARE FOR THE ENVIRONMENT

You love the outdoors and are willing to spend time caring for and helping preserve our natural assets. Our country has a lot of environment to care about. In fact, your area may be known for it. Look at your favorite natural area, park, forest, river, lake, watershed, or wildlife habitat and you'll find all types of groups who help preserve and protect it.

Options to give back to nature are plentiful. You'll find groups that adopt or friend their favorite community park, wildlife refuge, natural area, forest, river, wetlands, or garden. Connect with advocates who speak up and teach about nature. Volunteer with city, county, and parks departments who are eager to sign you up for park duty. Sign on with organizations in your own neighborhood that partner with cities and parks departments to keep parks healthy and safe.

Dig In, Clean Up, Party On!

Sign up for a work party. You can be part of a weekend or weekday (you're retired, remember) work group at a park, natural area, garden, or wildlife reserve. Unearth your boots, gloves and shovels to plant flowers, trees, and shrubs; pull weeds or build flower beds. Count birds and wildlife. Be an active learner and educate others on causes you are passionate about.

Organizations generally are flexible and will match your schedule to their activity. Choose a one-time project or clean-up or be on a regular volunteer schedule. Get dirty working outside or skip the dirt and mud and work in an office or an outreach program. Take photos, write for blogs and websites. It all makes a difference.

You'll take away the satisfaction of connecting with Mother Earth, doing your part to keep the world healthy, growing, and green. Along the way you'll meet new people and learn something new about your area's unique ecology. And don't forget how outdoor exercise benefits brain health! It is so very win-win.

There are many opportunities to dig deeper to find inspiration and information about the best places to join green teams in your area.

Friend or Adopt a Natural Area

Dedicated "friends of" and park stewardship groups everywhere work to preserve local and community parks and natural areas. Often, they team up with city or county parks organizations. Park warriors participate in park planning, clean up, work parties, identifying problems, and getting involved in park education and advocacy issues.

Most Friend groups are free or low-cost to join. Friend groups are perfect places to get your hands dirty, socialize, and learn more about park ecology. And get outdoors!

Look for activities you can enjoy with kids and grandkids. Guaranteed you'll be digging around with young old people like us.

Ecological Preservation Groups

These volunteer groups tackle environmental preservation in expansive and dramatic spaces of

rivers, watersheds, wetlands, and wildlife habitats. Examples include projects in forests that focus on the park's ecological health; many maintain trail systems. Volunteer jobs at wildlife refuges range from conducting tours to habitat restoration. Friends groups of large natural wonders work to preserve sprawling, complicated outdoor spaces and protect the scenic beauty though work parties, discovery hikes, and community education.

Volunteers at wetlands preserves help at education centers and on crews that remove invasive plants, maintain trails, and work with marshes. State affiliates of organizations such as the Nature Conservancy sponsor restoration projects that benefit natural areas in many states. (nature.org)

Advocacy and Education

If your passion is sharing knowledge, many environmental organizations welcome outreach and education volunteers. Many

ecological preservation groups advocate for their areas in public and political forums. Organizations such as the Sierra Club (sierraclub.org) get involved in the nitty gritty of Environmental Impact Statements and in influencing public policy decisions – legislative, legal, administrative, and electoral.

State-specific groups communicate with the public regarding political issues involving the public wildlands, wildlife, and waters. Outreach programs may also include workshops, classes, and models of environmental preservation in action at their sites.

Other local environmental nonprofits bring environmental education to the community through on-site education programs in schools and at community events

CHAPTER 8: CAREER ENCORES

While many Boomers eagerly trade jobs and career for a leisure retirement, others opt to stay in the workforce. An increasing number want or need to work for the money. Others do because they just plain enjoy their jobs, the daily routine, and their daily contact with co-workers. Not to mention they find their work satisfying and feel valued. Sometimes, it's just hard to let go.

Turning Points and Second Chances

Retirement age for many Boomers is a turning point. It's finally time to look elsewhere for a more meaningful career or job, or a better schedule or situation. Some prefer a gradual transition out of their jobs, working out part-time or consulting deals.

Still others are ready for a second chance to do what they love or fulfill their life purpose. For them, it's now-or-never time to realize an entrepreneurial dream and turn skills, experience and interests into a business or do independent work.

Change Careers, Profession, or Situation

Popular stay-in-the-workforce options among Boomers are:

- Transitioning to another role within an organization, applying expertise to areas such as training or mentoring.

- Shifting to a flexible or part-time schedule or working from a home office (or coffee shop).

- Moving to a similar position at a different organization within the same industry.

- Taking business skills and experience to a favorite nonprofit.

- Seeking out a new batch of education or training to pivot to an entirely different career, profession, or industry.

Where to Start the Process

Either within or outside your current situation, a good job search involves research and networking. The process starts by evaluating skills, experience and expertise, and defining an "ideal" job. Among the many parts of ideal are hours, work environment, location, work culture, interaction, projects, and compensation.

Research the types of industries and organizations that would be a good fit. Learn more through internet searches, talking with friends, acquaintances, and many others. Take advantage of the tools, resources, and people available to you, many at no or low cost.

Today's online world delivers job search guides, checklists, and other tools to your desktop or other devices. From building a resume to interviewing, to networking, to researching, it is all out there.

Resources for Career Change

Hands-on job seekers enroll in live and online classes and seminars at community colleges; many also coach. Companies and industry groups, and even AARP (aarp.org), sponsor job fairs and career classes.

Experts agree that networking – a skill Boomers naturally excel at – is the key to finding a new gig. It's easy to spread the word among networks of friends, acquaintances, former employers, workout buddies and many others. They are eager to help. Social media such as LinkedIn, Facebook, and other social media platforms are good ways to connect; use them in ways appropriate for you and your situation.

The following are examples of organizations that Boomers can tap into to land a new job.

- AARP. Jobs, Work & Resources by city. Job hunting articles and links to job hunting sites, niche sites, and social media. (aarp.org)

- AARP Tek Academy. An online connection to job search tools and online career fairs. (learn.aarp.org)

- Community Colleges. Check out your local community colleges for career and technical programs for career changes.

- Job search websites such as Career Builder, Career One Stop, Indeed, and Monster. Search for openings by location and job type.

CHAPTER 9: COMMUNITY SERVICE

In this chapter, community service refers to organizations that serve individuals, families, and youth facing challenges with addictions and mental health, food insecurity, homelessness, and other human issues.

Retirement is a great time to explore community service opportunities and give back to make our communities better places to live. Our

communities care deeply about the needs of health-challenged, less fortunate, and underserved populations. We want to help people out of the mainstream who are homeless, hungry or need other types of help.

Many community service organizations are nonprofit and depend heavily upon volunteers. Many are grass-roots groups and others are sponsored by churches and

civic groups. Many people – like you – start and run them. Volunteer roles are as varied as the organizations and need all types of skills, or just the desire to do whatever is needed to meet their client needs.

Types of Service Organizations

Look for a general category below that interests you and the types of services performed by volunteers. Then do research on specific organizations in your area and what types of help you could provide.

- **Addictions and Mental Health.** A wide variety of organizations serve the community through mental health treatment, education and support for adults, families, and children. Volunteers perform in many support roles such as mentoring, answering calls, development, communication, teaching, and helping at events.

- **Disability Services.** These organizations support adults and children with disabilities to help people realize their potential and provide opportunities in areas such as housing, recreation, fitness, daily living, transportation, and socializing. Volunteers assist with programs, camp activities, work parties, social events, learning and education, transportation, fundraising, and administrative support.

- **Emergency Services.** Emergency food, shelter and other services are provided to individuals and families by a variety of nonprofit, faith-based, and other agencies. Volunteers assist in shelters, food pantries, clothing rooms, and thrift stores; they serve meals, help with care and office tasks, drive, and teach.

- **Family and Social Services**. Many community organizations serve families through programs that address social issues such as abuse, relationship issues, illness, and financial problems. Volunteers help with client care tasks, education, work in all types of office roles.

- **Food Banks and Gardens**. Food pantries provide food for low-income individuals and families, and people who are homeless. Fresh food is grown at area gardens and provided to food banks. Volunteers help unpack, repackage, sort and box food, and serve clients. Garden and farm volunteers help plant, weed, harvest, and deliver fruits and vegetables to food banks. They also build gardens and teach people how to grow their own food.

- **Hunger and Homeless Services**. Resources for homeless people include shelters, meals, clothing, healthcare, training, transitional programs, and other services provided by nonprofits, faith-based, and government organizations. Volunteers help in shelters, prepare meals, interact with clients, help with child and animal care, staff clothing and food rooms, teach, and outreach and maintenance.

- **Youth Programs**. A variety of programs for all ages of youth offer opportunities to learn through sports, reading, writing, games, arts and crafts, music, and outdoor activities – many with emphasis on underserved populations. Volunteers help mentor, teach, and coach children, and help with trips and events, outreach, and fundraising.

CHAPTER 10: EVENTS, FESTIVALS

Events and festivals are a big part of any community's experience. We enjoy all flavors of festivals. Through festivals we celebrate our love for art, music, reading, theater, and our ethnicity. We also enjoy events and festivals around food and beverage, cars, nature, books, healthy living, being outdoors, sports, and many, many other interests.

We turn out for events that celebrate our cities, towns and communities, our holidays, and our sports. We get involved in large and small events that support causes in our communities. And we delight in events that are just plain fun and sometimes a touch weird.

While warmer seasons naturally bring more events and festivals, you'll find celebrations and events year around. New ones pop up all the time. Festivals and events are a perfect way to have healthy fun with friends and family and celebrate our communities.

Volunteers Wanted and Needed

If you've not done it before, look into a behind-the-scenes job at your favorite festival or event. Apply at least several months in advance to assure that you get a spot.

Centered around a special interest, festivals bring together a sponsoring organization, a team of planners, vendors, and lots of volunteers. With all the work involved to coordinate many moving pieces and parts, volunteers are essential and very welcome. For the event and festival volunteer groupies, opportunities are nearly endless.

Depending on the type, behind-the-scenes volunteers get involved much earlier in planning time and place logistics, working with sponsors, fundraising, and promoting the event.

Outdoor day-of-event roles vary widely from selling tickets and concessions, staffing information tables and booths, setting up stages, assisting with and coordinating activities, answering questions, assisting performers, and of course, cleanup!

You may also get to work with a favorite artist, performer, musician, athlete, or winemaker. Or you may get to hear music from the era of the old cars you're reminiscing about.

Sporting and Active Outdoor Events

What sports do you love? Soccer, baseball, track & field, running, tennis, and golf are only a few! Sporting events and local competition, whether for a school, college, professional or community event, offer may ways offer your support and enjoy the fun of competition.

One way to enjoy sports is combine your interest in the sport with a volunteer job. And…possibly land a free admission ticket! If you enjoy youth sports, look into a mentoring or coaching role in school and community sponsored programs. Or take on support tasks such as maintaining equipment, setting up competitive events, or selling items.

Consider also volunteering at other types of community sporting events such as run-walk and cycling events. Volunteers enjoy many interesting options from the logistics of months-in-advance planning, designing t-shirts and awards, working with sponsors, assembling goodie packets, setting up a course, handing out food or water on a course, staffing a finish line, and coordinating kids' events.

Find an event on your community calendar and check out its website. You'll have fun, meet other people, and enjoy the sense of community.

Farmers Markets

What could be healthier right? All that fresh food. Families walking. Homemade good-for-you products. People enjoying the summer outdoors in their community. Listening to bluegrass and just sometimes…classic rock.

Farmers markets need and welcome help in setting up and taking down the market, staffing an information booth, setting up signs, helping vendors, and many other behind the scenes and office chores.

Events and Festivals that Recruit Volunteers

If you need ideas, see the list below for types of festivals and events to add to your summer fun with family and friends. Most, if not all, need and welcome all types of volunteers. To find them, search on-line for community events or by event type and name of your community.

- Active/heathy living (cycle, run, walk)
- Animal adoption
- Art (outdoor fairs and festivals)
- Book fairs and publishing
- Cars and transportation
- City Celebrations
- Cultural and ethnic
- Farmers markets
- Food and beverage
- Holiday celebrations (4th of July, Memorial, Labor Day, Christmas)
- Out of the box weird (kite, garlic, mushroom)
- Music (all types)
- Special Interest (model trains, tractors, toys)
- Sports Events (professional, amateur, all types)
- Street and neighborhood
- Theater and performance, film

For lists of upcoming festivals and events, so check calendars of your city or community, Chamber of Commerce, parks and recreation programs, community organizations, sporting goods stores, or special interest groups that promote events.

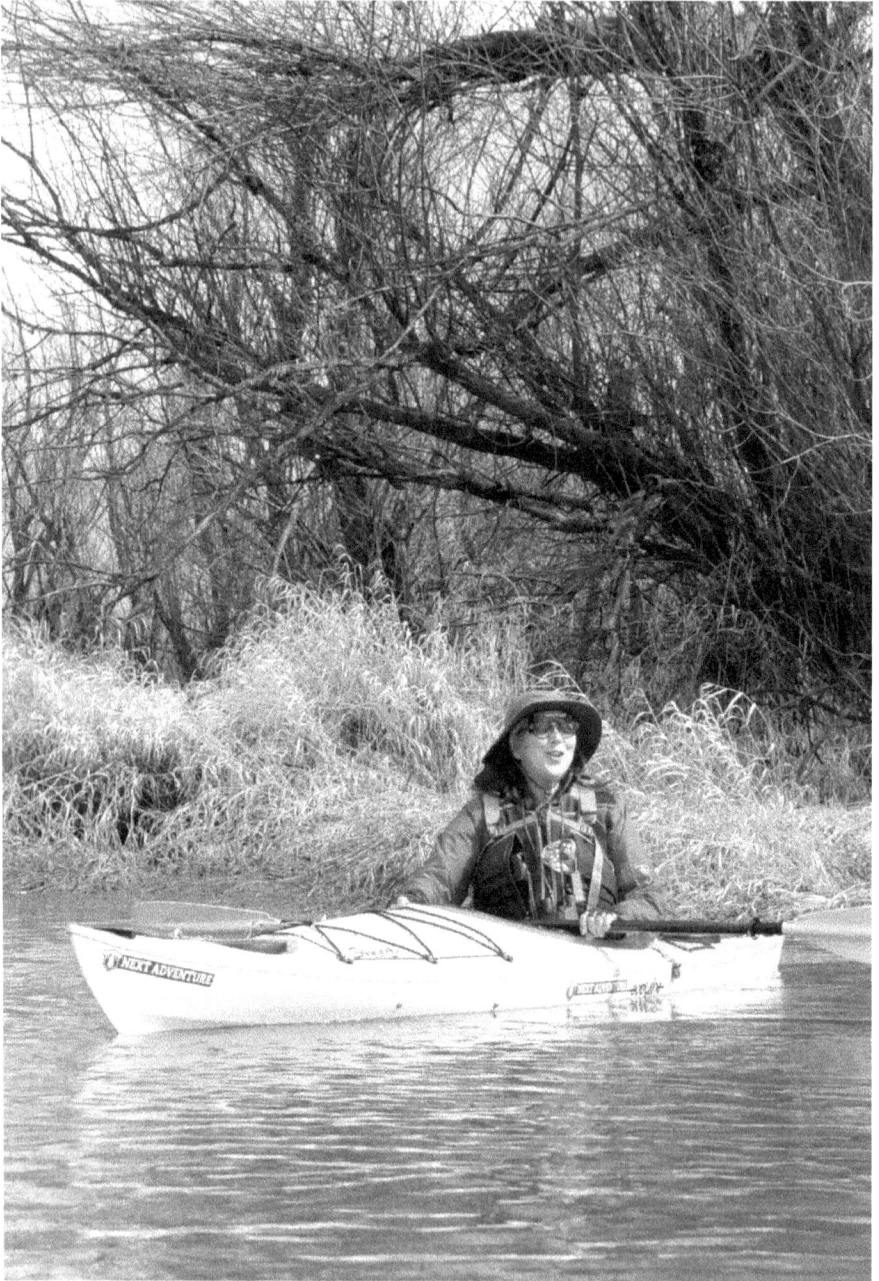

CHAPTER 11: FITNESS, HEALTHY LIVING

Boomers heading into their next chapters want to be healthy and fit enough to enjoy it. And the secret formula is really no secret – exercise and diet are the best "magic pills" we have for a healthy quality of life. And doing something fun for fitness with people we enjoy = a "super magic pill."

Exercise is essential because it strengthens our hearts and nourishes our brains. Being healthy and fit helps our mental fitness, balance, stamina, flexibility, strength, mobility, and ability to ward off disease. Boomers who exercise regularly feel better and can do more.

Already healthy and fit? Try a new activity to help keep you on track. Or, if you had a sedentary, butt-in-the seat job, look for a gradual program to start exercising. Try these three steps:

- Step One – Fit activity into your life by thinking about what activities you enjoy or always wanted to try. *Do you like the outdoors? Do you prefer being indoors for fitness classes or water exercise? Always wanted to dance? Play Golf? Garden, do yard work? Walk the dog? Paddle a kayak? Ski or snowshoe?*

- Step Two – Next think about your goals. *More energy, stamina to keep up with your spouse, friends, kids, or grandkids? Weight loss? Better body image? Improved quality of life? Better sleep? Make new friends?*

- Step Three – Scope out your options. Fitness opportunities – outdoor and indoor – surround Boomers in our own communities. Choices of places, programs and classes for your fitness quest are endless. Add the huge benefit, yes benefit, of age – many fitness activities are either free or discounted for adults and older adults. Look for them. Two of them – Silver&Fit® and SilverSneakers® – no cost fitness programs included in many senior health plans and group retirement plans.

Important advice from fitness experts is to continually challenge yourself in some small way and set goals. Goals can be a cycling distance, walking in an event, or taking on a ski or snowshoe trail.

Mix up your schedule with activities to experience something new, make friends, and boost the health benefits.

Now, check out our rundown of Boomer-popular, fun, and readily available fitness and exercise options below.

Walk, Hike, Ski, Snowshoe for Fitness

One of the easiest ways to start a fitness program is by walking. Get a good pair of walking shoes and comfortable socks and workout clothes. Join a group of like-minded people. Or find a walking buddy to keep you both on track.

Head out in your own neighborhood, taking in the scenery, the people and neighborhood parks and gardens. Step it up and venture to other neighborhoods. Or check out walking and hiking trails around town. Join a walking group or Meetup. Check a neighborhood's walk score (walkscore.com/score) which tells you how easy and safe it is to walk to shopping, recreation activities, and transportation.

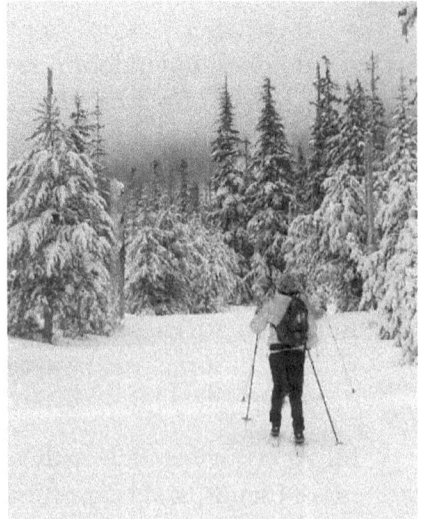

In winter, extend your local-motion to snow sports – join other retirees in fitness activities such as downhill, and cross-country skiing or snowshoeing or snowboarding. Check out the outdoor clubs and Meetups, or classes to find eager companions and group trips. In warmer climates, go north for snow in your favorite mountains, hills, forests, or flatlands. See also *CHAPTER 15: HIKING, WALKING* on page 85.

Cycling: Ride, Boomers, Ride!

Ready to cycle into your next phase of leisure living? It's a popular way to experience outdoor activity with family and friends, exercise, or just enjoy the calming peace of a solo ride.

Good news – you need look no further than your own community. Thanks to bicycle advocacy groups and transportation programs, city and county planning in many communities encourages bicycling both as recreation and transportation. Check out your area's cycling options including bike lanes, multi-use trails, and off-road trail riding options. Cycle around town, in commuter lanes to work, and side roads. Learn to trail ride. Or sign-up for community biking events and rides.

Places to Bike, Maps

Start by search on these sites:

- Rails to Trails Conservancy, an on-line source for 30,000 trail maps, searchable by location. (TrailLink.com)

- Mapmyride.com, allows you to search for bike routes by community.

- The department of transportation websites of your city, county, and state, parks and recreation programs, and bike shops.

Cycling Clubs, Events, Meetups

No matter where you hang your helmet, or whether you are a recreational to competitive cyclist, there's a club or group for you. Meetups (meetup.com), groups formed around a single interest, are a popular option for Boomers seeking all things outdoors, including cycling. And cycling events of all sizes and types are plentiful throughout the country.

Running, Jogging

Are you still jogging along, no doubt a bit slower than you did in the running craze of the 60s, 70s and 80s? Or is jogging/running for fitness on your bucket list? How about a 5K? 10K? Marathon? Aerobic activities such as jogging and running raise your heart rate and are important to good heart health and brain fitness. Start with a good pair of running shoes, comfortable socks, and workout clothes (no cotton!) and get moving. You can jog practically anywhere. Prefer some company? Show up for group runs sponsored by a club or local running store. Look into running meetups. Most clubs welcome all abilities, and you'll have plenty of company no matter what your pace.

Put a 5K or 10K event on the calendar. Running events attract hundreds and even thousands of joggers, runners, and walkers of all shapes, sizes, and abilities. Many Boomers jog with their kids and grandkids. Most races are family friendly with kids' races and walks. What's not to like about them? It's also wise to look into group training sessions that help prepare you for a race.

For more information, check the websites of local running and walking clubs, or visit these websites to find one in your area:

- runningintheusa.com. A website where you can search for local event schedules by city. Find one and sign up. Register on-line.

- Road Runners Club of America, search for a club by state. (rrca.org/find-a-running-club)

On the Water

Water sports are a great way to enjoy our connection to water and experience the amazing scenic waterways in our country. Water sports offer many opportunities for exercise and fun (or serious!) competition. Especially popular ways to do both (or not) are the row sports of canoeing, kayaking, dragon boating, and sculling.

Kayak and Canoeing

Kayaking and canoeing offer gentle ways to enjoy experience the nooks and crannies of nature up close in lakes, rivers, coastlines, and other waterways. These fresh air sports are easily enjoyed with family and friends, especially grandkids.

Dragon Boating

Enthusiasts tell us that once you've tried it, there's no turning back. Dragon boating teams compete on their own circuit throughout the country. In some communities, over-55 paddlers can join their own dragon boat team for fun and fitness. It's been said that they openly claim that old age and treachery will overcome youth and ambition. (You'll have to see for yourself, of course.)

Paddle, Scull, Row

Paddle boarding has been the rage most currently but sculling and sweeping are gaining fans. Sculling is another rowing sport popular in many waterways. In sculling, 1 to 8 people propel a scull by rowing with two oars, often in competition. Sweep rowing involves a pair of rowers, each using a single oar.

How to Start

You can get involved in paddling and rowing sports either on your own or in a group. Classes for all ages and abilities are conducted by community outfitters, city parks programs, community colleges, and other organizations.

Clubs are another way to acquaint yourself with the paddle and row sports and find kindred spirits. Whether you are a beginner or looking for white water adventure, there's a club here for you.

Visit the websites of your area's kayaking, canoeing and paddling clubs to find information about lessons and events. At the same time, find opportunities to share what you know about your favorite paddling sports by teaching or coaching, or volunteering at an event.

Just Keep Swimming

Boomer swimmers love the gentle all-body workout water exercise gives them, making swimming a popular year-around fitness activity. Lap swims, lessons, and water exercise are available at aquatic centers, parks and recreation facilities, community colleges, and public swimming pools. Not to mention lakes, rivers, and beaches. Exercise pools are also a common amenity for residents of retirement communities.

Tennis or Pickleball Anyone?

Tennis and pickleball are each fun, fit-friendly and social activities that go beyond just moving exercise. Racket sports connect your brain, and eyes to your racket hand and then hopefully to the ball. To keep relationships harmonious, you can partner with, instead of against, a spouse or friend.

Pickleball has become a wildly popular sport among Boomers. Much like tennis, players hit balls over a net on a smaller court. A solid paddle and a ball much like a whiffle ball slow things down.

Get lessons through many community programs and find classes, schedules, and other Boomer players at activities sponsored by parks and recreation programs, and pickleball and tennis organizations and facilities.

Golf, of Course!

Tired of driving past beautiful, lush, expansive golf courses on your way to work? Is dreamland taking you to an early round, where you breathe in fresh air, exercise, and enjoy buddy banter.

Wait no longer! you're retired, or soon to be, right? It's time to trade the laptop for a five-wood and hit the fairways (at least as many of them as possible). So, do it now, especially if learning or playing more golf is a bucket list item.

Hundreds of communities around the country are golf wonderlands for everyone – from beginner to old pros alike. Courses range from tour class to forest and farmlands-bordered hills, to ocean-hugging links, to mountain backdrop cactus fields, in large and small towns, and everything in between.

Never swung a club? Many golf courses and clubs offer all levels of instruction and rental equipment. To find a course near you, search for courses in your community, or state golf associations. Golf classes also are offered through parks and recreation programs and community colleges. (And friends or your spouse, of course, will eagerly offer you much welcomed advice.)

Golf Volunteers

If you enjoy the fresh air and fun of attending tournaments, look for opportunities to volunteer at one. You'll get a free pass to walk with your favorite golfers, along with helping others enjoy the experience. Check tournament schedules at golf organizations in your community and contact the golf course hosting the event for information.

Volunteers also can help others learn and enjoy golf. Opportunities are available with many state associations to help with adult and junior golf tournaments, and administrative duties within the state. The First Tee organization, for example, relies on volunteers to carry out its mission in many states – to introduce the game to young people.

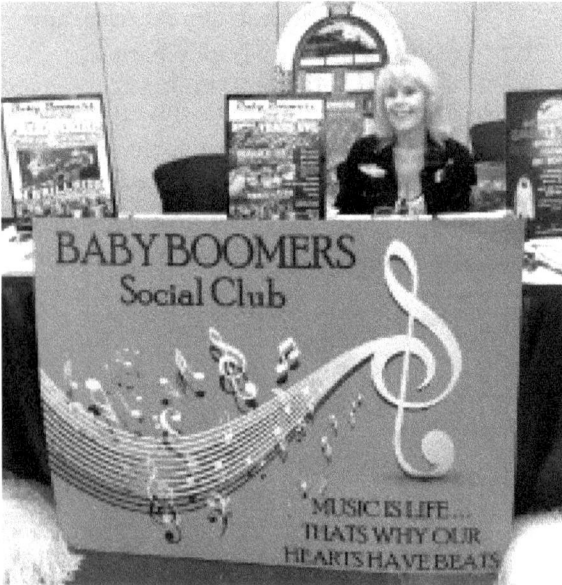

Shall We Dance?

Remember when Boomers twisted, watusied, hitchhiked, strolled, loco-motioned, hully-gullied, mashed potatoed, discoed, and hustled though the 60s and 70s? Today, Boomers find their way back to all forms of old as well as new dance floor moves from ballroom and country to contra and Latin, and everything in between.

Can you guess why? To stay fit, learn something new, meet new people, and for the best reason, bring back those fun times.

For places to break out your unique dance style or learn distinct dances, look for websites of community retirees' or social clubs, private dance studios, or dance Meetups or clubs. Many ethnic organizations teach their signature folk dances, a fun way to socialize. Other places to practice vintage and modern dances are community colleges, community and senior centers, and parks and recreation classes.

Join a Senior or Community Center

Health and fitness – both physical and mental – are a main focus of senior centers, community centers, and YMCAs that gear activities to different ages, abilities, and interests.

Senior centers offer services and activities to help seniors live, learn, thrive, and socialize. Depending on the community, retirees can take advantage of fitness classes in strength training, dance, aerobics, Tai Chi, yoga, and other popular exercises. Many offer classes and activities related to lifestyle, health and nutrition, and post schedules of free or low-cost classes on their website.

More Choices: Community College, Parks Programs

In addition to community centers, retirees can sign up for a wide range of fitness classes offered by community colleges, and parks and recreation departments of their cities. For descriptions and schedules, check their websites and current activities catalog.

Find Healthy Lifestyles at Healthcare Organizations

Healthcare organizations around the country promote healthy living through classes and events in their communities. Many provide online classes and videos. Ongoing, popular classes may include healthy eating, fitness and exercise, weight management, smoking cessation, support groups, stress management, pain management, depression, yoga, and many other health topics related to retirees and seniors.

Fitness Activities Meetups

No matter what your fitness level or interest, there's a club or Meetup group for you. Meetups are formed by individuals around common or multiple interests, in this case fitness and exercise. Joining is either free or inexpensive and gives you online access to the Meetup's scheduled activities. Search Meetups in your area at meetup.com.

CHAPTER 12: GARDENING

Got a little dirt under your nails? Have a need to pluck weeds and water flowers? If so, there's probably a gardener growing in you!

Look around. Seems like everyone either wants to start or spend more time in a garden, for good reason. Gardening grounds us. Clears our brains. Expresses our creativity. Gives us solitude. And makes us patient.

If you're a Boomer gardener or want-to-be, it's time to unearth gloves and shovels, and get to the garden of your choice. Most communities are garden friendly to beginners and experts alike – gardeners love to share their knowledge.

Enjoy Public and Demonstration Gardens

Start by venturing out to see all the luscious gardens that bless your area (and beyond). Some public, some private by invitation. Then bring your inspiration back in photographs to start applying those ideas to your own yard, containers, patio, or balcony.

Whether you're a beginner, expert, or appreciator, you'll discover endless ways to enjoy gardens in parks, botanical gardens, wildlife areas, public buildings, university campuses, and many other places unique to your state, city, or county.

Gather inspiration by wandering through demonstration gardens in your areas that offer the latest on new plants, trees, and growing techniques. Depending on where you live, you'll find places that focus on fruit growing, organic gardening, and gardens as wildlife habitat, as well as techniques to manage factors such as water usage, soil enhancement, and safety.

Volunteer at a Public Garden

All public gardens need and welcome volunteers of all skill levels and interests. Great for beginners! Tasks range from hands-on planting, weeding, and mulching, to helping at special events, or working in gift shops or offices. You can show up at one-time work parties or join others in ongoing year-round maintenance. Some branch out into community and youth learning projects.

Take volunteering a step further and join a friends group that adopts and maintains their favorite public garden.

Community Gardens

When you enjoy growing things, but lack space to plant your personality, you've probably discovered community gardens. You enjoy the satisfaction of beautiful flowers or healthy vegetables and meeting others with the same interests. Share tips, seeds, and even recipes.

Carry that a step further, and help others enjoy gardening by teaching, speaking or volunteering.

Most communities offer residents garden plots and various gardening equipment and services for gardeners. By volunteering to teach or provide gardening tips, you'll enrich your own experience by helping others learn what you love.

Garden volunteers with a community service interest should check out organizations that help people grow their own food. Volunteers help build organic, raised bed vegetable gardens in yards, and balconies, or volunteer time in food growing orchards and gardens that donate fresh food to food banks. Some offer tool-sharing. Can't find a community garden? Start one!

Garden Clubs

Garden clubs are a fun, social way to learn and share information on all things gardening and to also enhance the beauty of your community. Garden clubs offer opportunities to share your knowledge as a speaker or help put on workshops, plant shows, plant sales and exchanges, and garden tours. Some clubs offer scholarships for aspiring horticulturalists as well as donate goods and time to local charities.

Members also maintain flower beds in their cities, and encourage the appreciation of wildflowers, birds, insects, and the wise use of natural resources. Moreover, members share the fellowship of like-minded gardening enthusiasts.

For more information, search for garden clubs in your area. They may be affiliated with a state association and listed on its website. Garden clubs typically welcome all aspiring green thumbs and are eager to help and share their knowledge.

Gardening Classes, Workshops, Seminars

Gardening for most of us is evolutionary – there's always more to learn. Discover new design, seeds, soils, watering, plants, color, harvest – it goes on and on. And there's no shortage of places to learn more, get advice, attend classes and seminars, and hang out with other gardeners.

To really dig into gardening, attend Master Gardener classes typically offered through state universities. They often cater to the serious gardener who in turn, shares their knowledge through gardening-related demonstrations, lectures, seminars, and workshops in communities throughout their state.

Other options are community education gardening classes typically held in spring and fall. Search for gardening classes offered through

community colleges. Nurseries and garden centers also hold gardening classes and hands-on workshops.

Home and garden shows are still another source of classes and workshops to inspire and educate gardeners.

Also, look for garden clubs that invite the public to their classes. Community gardens also sponsor classes for those who want a healthy, thriving, and successful planting.

Like to share your knowledge? Contact your favorite garden club, public or community gardens, community college, community or senior center, or nurseries to teach a class. For places to attend classes or ideas or places to share your knowledge, see *CHAPTER 24: TEACHING, SPEAKING* on page 111.

Green Thumb Groups

Boomer gardeners should check out gardening groups or Meetup groups (meetup.com). Meetups are formed by individuals around a common, or multiple interests, in this case, gardening. Joining is either free or inexpensive and gives you on-line access to the Meetup's scheduled activities.

CHAPTER 13: GOVERNMENT SERVICE

Do you enjoy an active interest in your local government?

Are you interested in being part of discussions and decisions affecting your community's parks, public safety, or art and cultural events and activities?

Many community-minded Boomers are and find that joining a county or city board, committee, or commission is a rewarding experience.

Boards and commissions advise city and county agencies and bureaus on community issues and policies. They value the experience and the variety of expertise that retirees and seniors bring to the local governing process.

Counties and cities stress the importance of citizen advisors who represent the full range of diversity in their communities.

Volunteers can opt to serve on standing committees or citizen advisory groups that deal with specific issues. Websites of each county and city describe the functions and the makeup of their boards, committees, and commissions, including how to apply. Many counties and cities also have committees for citizen involvement that focus on getting diverse groups of citizens active in government processes.

Regional Government

In large metropolitan areas, government entities with regional jurisdiction provide regionwide planning and coordination to manage growth, infrastructure, and development issues that cross jurisdictional boundaries. They may get involved in: regional research; management of parks, trails and natural areas; transportation; large-scale visitor venues such as zoos and convention centers; performing arts theaters; and utilities such as solid waste and recycling facilities.

Members of the community serve on various committees that shape public policies, transportation, funding, and more. Learn about current opportunities by visiting the advisory committees, citizen involvement, or the volunteer pages of the government website. You also may find information on other types of volunteer opportunities at facilities they manage, such as parks, theater, and entertainment venues.

County Government

Citizen volunteers in county government take active roles in shaping policies, programs, and decisions supporting specific county activities and goals. Advisory boards and committees deal with areas such as aging, animal control, bicycle and pedestrian safety, libraries, budgets, clean water, historic preservation, parks, public health, arts, building codes, telecommunications, tourism, traffic safety, and more.

Individual counties typically offer opportunities based on the unique features of its community. For information, visit the citizen involvement or volunteer pages of your county website.

City Government

Citizen volunteers serve on boards and commissions much like those of counties. Depending on the city, citizen committees support parks and recreation, city-owned facilities, budgets, architectural review, libraries, planning, arts and culture, tourism, citizen involvement, finance, water, zoning, public safety, transportation, and utilities.

Boards and commissions play a critical role in supporting city functions and advising the city leaders on a variety of issues and topics. Cities find that citizen involvement is essential to incorporating the community's voice in city decision-making.

For information, visit the citizen involvement or volunteer pages of your city's website.

Law Enforcement Volunteers

Many communities need volunteers in special law enforcement programs involving various safety, parks, and outreach programs. For example, volunteers may participate in bike safety projects and community outreach crafts and games. In some communities, police volunteers help with car seat clinics, clerical duties, home security, and similar programs.

Another program some communities offer is a reserve officer program which trains volunteers for uniformed, armed duties or non-uniform, unarmed duties.

For information, visit the law enforcement or police department pages of your city's website.

Other Local Government Opportunities

Other areas within your local government that may welcome office volunteers include city attorneys, events at government owned facilities such as theaters, and special community projects and events such as a city-sponsored festival.

Other popular places to volunteer with city and county managed areas are parks and recreation departments and libraries. For more information, see *CHAPTER 25: THE GREAT OUTDOORS* on page 117 and *CHAPTER 18: LITERARY ARTS, READING, WRITING* on page 93.

Federal Government

Through the website Volunteer.gov, you can search for a variety of volunteer assignments with Federal government agencies and their state and local governmental partners. Its purpose is to provide an efficient way to connect volunteers with volunteer opportunities within natural and cultural resources agencies.

One popular activity among retirees who enjoy RVing, camping, and meeting new people, is working as a volunteer campground host at Federal facilities. Hosts stay at site in their camper or RV, and provide visitor information, recreation planning, and help with maintaining facilities. Opportunities are available throughout the country.

CHAPTER 14: HEALTHCARE VOLUNTEERING

Are you interested in using your healthcare or caregiving experience to a volunteer role? Or just interested in volunteering in healthcare?

Boomers who have retired from healthcare careers, or those interested in healthcare, can find a wide assortment of places and ways to offer their help in an area with many volunteer opportunities. Your involvement is welcomed by all types of medical and healthcare organizations, including these described below.

Community Healthcare

Nonprofit community health clinics bring low-cost or free healthcare to underserved, disadvantaged, low-income populations, the elderly, families, children, and others.

Often working with limited budgets, these organizations depend heavily on volunteers with medical and non-medical skills for day-to-day operations. Professionals such as doctors, nurses, clinicians, dentists, technicians are always needed, as are volunteers who serve as medical advocates, screeners, interpreters, and translators. Also welcome is a background in office support, technology and computers, graphic design, communication, fundraising, as well as other skills.

Community Mental Health

Community Mental Health nonprofits serve the mentally ill, as well as adults and children with addictions. These organizations are supported by private and faith-based organizations, and city and county governments. Specialties include family and individual mental health and addictions.

Volunteer opportunities range from mental health professionals and those who assist them, to childcare, education, manning crisis phone lines and socializing in residential facilities. Volunteers also work in office settings, gardens, thrift stores and at special events.

Health-based Organizations

These familiar organizations focus on advancing cures and treatment of a specific condition or disease, and services and support for people and families affected by the disease. Examples of organizations that support the people and families afflicted by disease include the American Cancer Society, American Heart Association, MS Society, and Alzheimer's Association, all with local chapters. Examples of other conditions addressed by support organizations are diabetes, hearing, blindness, Asperger's syndrome, brain injuries, Down syndrome, and muscular dystrophy.

Retirees often choose organizations that speak to their hearts – the disease or condition may have touched them or their families or friends. Organizations seek volunteers in roles that support their mission and activities. In general, volunteers help provide services, educate the public, and raise money. Many sponsor large community fundraising events and need lots of volunteers to put on the events.

They also work in office roles, maintain databases, file, and answer phones. On the communications side, volunteers may help with websites, social media, graphic design, photography, and writing assignments. Many work at large and small community fundraising events where they are involved in planning, outreach, setup, engaging with participants, operating information booths, and cleanup.

Hospice and End of Life Care

Volunteers provide important services to hospice organizations and the people they serve. Whether providing companionship to a person in the final months and weeks of life, offering support to family and caregivers, or helping with community outreach and fundraising, the contributions of volunteers are essential to the important work provided by hospice programs.

Every hospice relies on volunteer support to provide excellent end-of-life care to each patient and family. In fact, Medicare requires that a portion of patient care time be provided by volunteers.

Hospitals and Medical Centers

By this time in our lives, most Boomers are no strangers to medical centers. We often recall the kindness of volunteers who showed us to a room or brought us flowers or a newspaper. Volunteers bring joy to people at stressful times. Most hospitals offer volunteer positions throughout their operations.

Duties of hospital volunteers vary widely depending upon the facility. Volunteers may work in staff reception areas and gift shops, file and retrieve documents and mails, take out trash, clean up after nurses and doctors, provide administrative backup, assist with research, help visitors, visit with patients or transport various small items such as flowers, gifts and cards from unit to unit.

Other "advanced volunteers" are those who work on health care teams and are given special training to work with patients. They are more common in large hospitals, particularly university-affiliated and teaching hospitals.

The best source of information on volunteering with healthcare organizations typically is the volunteer page of their website.

If you've worked in a medical field, what types of knowledge and skill could you offer to a nonprofit healthcare organization?

Do you have a special interest in organizations that address various health conditions such as cancer, heart disease, and dementia? What are the opportunities in your community?

Would you like to volunteer to help patients and their families in a hospital setting – working in a gift shop, transporting people in wheelchairs, delivering papers, or giving directions, for example?

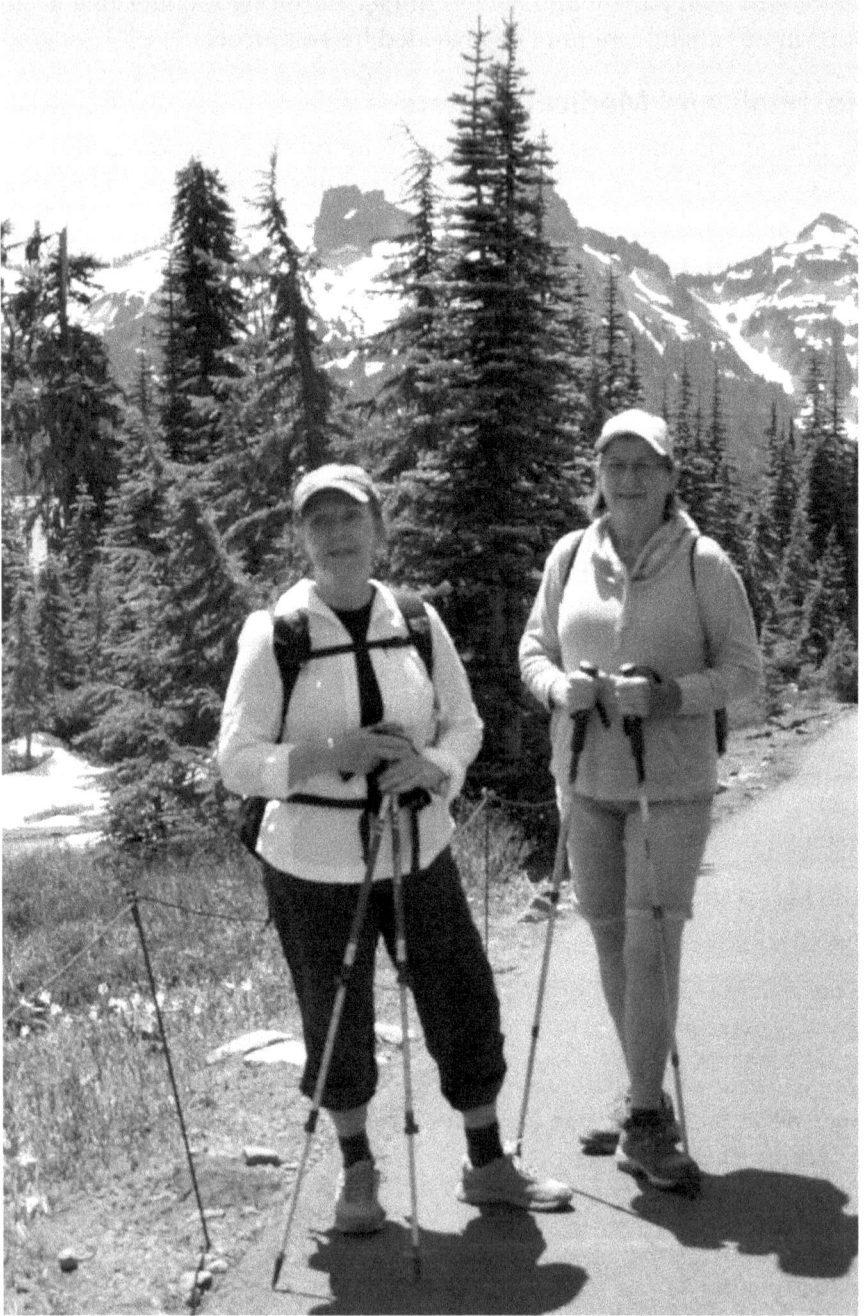

CHAPTER 15: HIKING, WALKING

Why are hiking and walking retirees' exercises of choice?

Easy – they are abundantly good for you and opportunities are plentiful. Nearly unlimited places to hike and walk in many communities make it easy and enjoyable to get your recommended weekly 150 walking minutes.

Multi-taskers can bundle walking with other leisure goals and hobbies. Pare down that paunch, give your partner space, feed your brain, or listen to nature. Explore communities beyond your own; discover out-of-the-way parks, trails, and fun little towns. Surround yourself with real forests and mountains, rivers, and wetlands. Make hikes and walks an excuse to see more of your family and friends or meet new people. Or just lose yourself or connect with nature in meditative hiking.

And – good news here – you needn't always traipse about a forest, park, or mountain trail to reap great health, aesthetic, and social benefits. Look for interesting urban or historic hiking routes and walkable neighborhoods, maybe your own!

Hike the Neighborhood

Not sure where to start? Get a good pair of walking shoes, comfortable socks, and workout clothes. Find a walking buddy to keep you both on track. Head out into your own neighborhood. Take in the scenery, the people, and the tucked away neighborhood parks and gardens. Gradually step it up and venture to other communities. In many areas, you can check a neighborhood's walk score which tells you its "walkability." (walkscore.com/score)

As you gather confidence, gather your friends, pick a destination, then download a map for a favorite, or new destination and head out.

Get Outside Your Home Zone

To find interesting explorable neighborhoods beyond your own, check out your city's (possibly a transportation page) or local parks and recreation website for maps and other information about walkable neighborhoods. Other sources of maps include the websites of outdoor, walking, or hiking clubs and meetups, outdoor stores, and local walking safety programs.

Other interesting walking options are mapped, informational walks through historic sites, neighborhoods, cities, or sections of cities. They typically explore an area's history and culture. Look for these on the websites of history organizations, cities, or visitor organizations. Or check out the website of local Volkssport groups which offer events and mapped routes to enjoy at your own pace.

Bird lovers find birding an enjoyable way to walk and observe the diverse habitats and habits of their feathered friends. Look for outings sponsored by local Audubon groups, parks programs, and community centers.

Step Out with a Club or Meetup Group

Age-friendly outdoor clubs and Meetups everywhere welcome non-members. Most offer different levels of activity and are a good way to meet like-minded Boomers. Many schedule activities during weekdays at times preferred by retirees. Many clubs offer multi-activities such as hiking, walking, snowshoeing, cycling, kayaking, and backpacking.

Community Walks

In many communities, you can choose from a few to dozens of walking and walker-friendly events. Some are multi-sport, multi-distance family events such as running races and fundraisers. Walk and multiply the benefits – your registration supports community causes, and you get exercise, camaraderie, an event t-shirt, and freebies.

Art and Cultural Meanderings

Add a little cultural variety to your walk. Log your miles when you show up for "first-something" art walks or stroll through regular or seasonal art walks held in many communities. Look on your city's website for routes and public spaces where you can experience art up close and personal.

You'll also get your steps in on guided or self-guided tours of historical sites, homes, buildings, farms, and gardens. Similarly, take advantage of events at expansive walk-around attractions in places such as arboretums, botanical gardens, nature parks, and zoos, as well as community sponsored food, art, brew, and wine walks.

Community College and City Recreation Programs

Browse the catalogs of your area's community colleges and city parks and recreation organizations for a wide variety of seasonal outdoor senior programs and walk and hike activities. Online sign-up is easy. Popular among retirees are hikes, walks, walk tours, nature and historic tours, nature center visits, and similar activities.

CHAPTER 16: HOBBIES

Research tells us that engaging in a creative or fun hobby tops the list of best activities for your brain. Maybe, now that we have the opportunity, it's time to move that hobby up the list.

Are you ready to express yourself with oil or watercolor? Start or expand a 60s record collection, make jewelry, take photos, drag out old bins of scrapbook material? What about restoring – toys, a car, furniture? Or building a model train track?

You might like to visit quaint antique shops of antiques. Sell stuff on eBay. Write a blog, memoir, or your family history. Learn the guitar or mandolin. Or build or restore one. Create or expand a garden. Express your out-of-the-box side with rock balancing, pigeon racing, blacksmithing, or beekeeping. There are endless possibilities.

Hobbies sprout from any interest – something you make, build, create, engage in, collect, fix, read, or learn about. Maybe it's a sport, art, music, books, history, an outdoor pursuit. By yourself or in a group, or both.

Where to Start

Searching in our digital world brings almost unlimited information and how-to videos right to your computer or phone screen. Search by hobby name and city and see what pops up. Other good places are hobby shops.

Most of your favorite learning places offer both in-person and online instruction and classes. Some examples are:

- Arts and Cultural Centers. Look into community's cultural center(s) for classes in all forms of art, crafts, music, theater, performance, dance, history, and more.

- Community College Continuing Education. Many offer classes on a wide spectrum of life-long learning interests including art and crafts, music, cooking, dancing, photography, reading, language, sports, woodworking, and more. Find out more in seasonal print or online catalogs.

- Community and Senior Centers. These friendly places are built around hobbies such as reading, dancing, card playing, arts, crafts, exercise, fitness, computers and technology, sports, and day trips. Groups always welcome beginners and are eager to share knowledge.

- Libraries. In addition to hobby books and media, libraries sponsor a variety of usually-free in-person and online programs on all sorts of hobby topics. Or you can suggest a class, or even teach one.

- Meetups, Clubs and Social Groups. People in these groups share a common interest. From arts, hobbies and crafts, to writing, culture, DIY, and many other activities, Meetups might be the place to look.

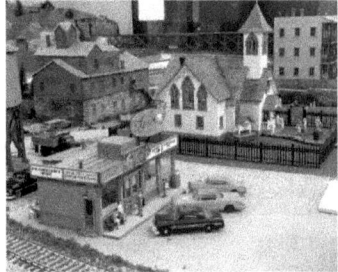

- Online Sources. Online classes on the hobby of your interest will bring you abundance information. Websites such as YouTube.com provide a wide selection of how-to videos on every imaginable hobby topic. See also the websites of retailers of hobby supplies, and hobby enthusiast organizations. Or create your own online class or workshop.

- Parks and Recreation Programs. Check the quarterly activities calendars of area parks programs for adult and senior group classes and activities such as creative arts, crafts, music, dance, bird watching, outdoor activities, games, sports, history, travel, and many more.

Depending on your interests, other ways to pursue hobbies are classes at cultural institutions such as art galleries, museums, and literary organizations, and programs sponsored by outdoor organizations and hobby supply stores.

Need Ideas? Start with our handy *Hobbies for You* download at boomersontheloose.com.

CHAPTER 17: LEARN SOMETHING NEW

There's no limit to what you can learn, and there's no limit to where you can find what you want. Most communities offer opportunities that transcend degree chasing and focus on more expansive interests that you might never find in a traditional classroom.

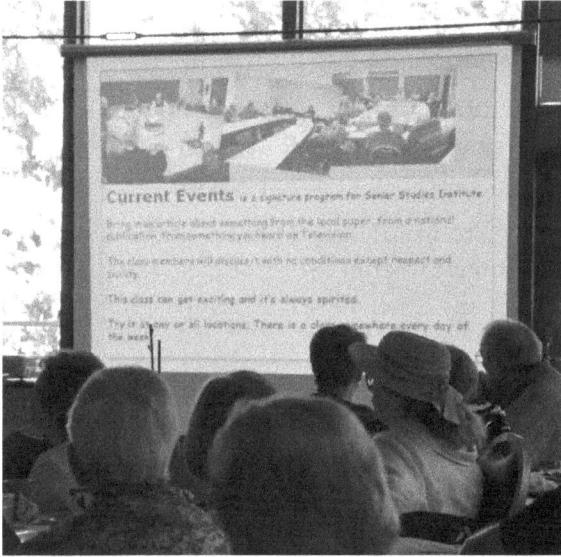

What challenges your mind in your world?

Current events, some historical curiosity, some unexplored mystery of life? Now that you have more time, your interests may turn to learning more about topics that fascinate you in your country, state, or community.

Online Learning

In recent times, computer learning has expanded rapidly, opening learners to more opportunities and a wide choice of topics available online. Feeding the popularity of online learning are the convenience of learning from a home computer. Many common learning and teaching forums have created and rapidly expanded learning programs via popular devices such as computers, phones, and tablets.

Your Library

Starting with library systems in their communities, Boomers discover abundant learning opportunities. Today's libraries host classes and workshops, author readings, art shows, cultural festivals, lectures, and abundant hands-on learning opportunities for all ages. Multi-library city or county systems make it easy for patrons to borrow materials in all multiple viewing formats from any library in their system.

More Learning Forums

Other low- or no-cost learning forums in your community include:

- Adult and Senior Enrichment Programs. These programs typically are sponsored by community colleges and universities and offer retirees a wide variety of in-person and online classes ranging from health fitness, current events, local history, and many others.

- Community Colleges. Local colleges offer credit and non-credit community education classes, both in-person and on-line, covering a wide spectrum of learning interests and current events. Find out more in seasonal catalogs available on-line or in print.

- College and University Lectures. In many communities, public and private colleges and universities invite the public to attend both in-person and online lectures, classes, and cultural events.

- Meetups, Clubs and Social Groups. People in most of these groups share a common learning interest. From arts, hobbies, and crafts, to writing, culture, DIY, and many other topics, Meetups offer many learning opportunities.

- Museums and Historical Societies. Museums are another place to pursue learning, especially for history buffs. Most museums offer a variety of programs, both in-person and on-line, about the history behind their collections.

- Parks and Recreation. The seasonal lineups of city parks and recreation programs also offer a wide variety of educational programs and classes that may be of interest. See their seasonal schedules or website for class descriptions and schedules.

- Retiree Living Communities. One of the amenities offered at the growing number of retirement communities is a wide array of classes to learn more about current events, history, hobbies, the local area, and far more.

- Retiree Organizations. Other places to "never stop learning" are retiree organizations and groups. Many invite guest speakers on current topics. Check the website of your former employer or their retirees' organization.

- Senior and Community Centers. Many community and senior centers hold regular classes and special workshops on a variety of educational and historical topics.

For more information, visit the websites of these learning centers in your community.

CHAPTER 18: LITERARY ARTS, READING, WRITING

Two popular interests that Boomer retirees engage in more are reading and writing. That shouldn't surprise us because we enjoy more leisure time. We want to experience new lands, worlds, and even galaxies

through books. We want to better understand our changing, complex world, current events, our communities, and the human journey.

And thanks to ever-growing technology, new books, and authors in every genre stream to us. We can instantly order, borrow, and download books on any subject, direct from bookstores and libraries to our computers, readers, or listening device.

On the flip side, many retirees are fulfilling their dreams to write. Whether crafting a memoir or coming of age story, a sci-fi, romance, fantasy or time travel, or non-fiction reference guide, Boomers are taking up their pens and keyboards to release their creativity, imagination, and desire to learn, grow, and help others.

Public Libraries: Retiree Reader Heaven

Many Boomers and retirees find their "reading heaven" at their local libraries. Far from becoming extinct due to technology, libraries have thrived, evolving into interconnected digital-age facilities. These virtual and community centers of learning have become inter-generational, multi-cultural gathering places, with 24-hour Internet access to places far and wide.

Starting with major library systems throughout areas large and small, Boomer readers discover abundant reading opportunities. Boomers still show up at libraries to learn, look up stuff and, yes, check out dear-to-our-souls printed books. And, just maybe for convenience, download digital books.

Beyond books, today's libraries feature art shows, gardens, and sculptures. They host cultural events, operate bookstores, provide computer and Wi-Fi services, home delivery, conference rooms, and a variety of community services.

Helping Others Learn

Libraries need curious people like you who are interested in helping people learn in one of your favorite places. Volunteers in today's libraries bring a wide variety of skills and interests to match the ever-expanding services libraries provide.

Beyond housing book and media collections, library programs help kids learn to read, seniors find services and adults navigate computers. Libraries need lots of volunteers – from teens to adults and seniors – who help throughout library operations. For example, they assist in computer labs, help put on public events and represent the library to the community. Inside, they shelve books, check in materials, assist patrons, perform office and administrative tasks, teach classes, work with books, help in after-school and summer programs, and arts and crafts classes.

Many volunteers are multi-lingual, and if you have diverse language skills, you're in demand!

Library Friends

Library "Friends" groups support their libraries for charitable, literary, and educational purposes. They help to raise money to support literacy projects as well as for day-to-day operations. They help build library collections, purchase equipment, work in bookstores, and support activities such as summer reading programs. Another plus for Boomers, Friends groups are just that – a place to make new friends.

Other Libraries

Public libraries aren't the only places to express your interest in books, reading, or helping others learn. Many other types of organizations house their own library collections and rely on volunteers to make books easy to find, use and return.

The collections at art, history, and other types of cultural centers may be organized and managed by volunteers who blend organizational skills with their art or cultural interest. Library volunteers in retirement communities use their expertise to build and manage a collection for residents (usually based on donations), so that books are easy to find.

You can use your interest in books and libraries in other ways too. Self-styled "mini-libraries" housed in little structures commonly pop up in neighborhoods or on front porches where residents can exchange books easily. Volunteers at nonprofit thrift stores and faith communities may need help organizing their book donations so they're easy to browse through.

Other Connections with Books

In addition to libraries, Boomers may have access to other fun connections with books. Some of the most common come through book clubs, reader events at libraries and bookstores, author readings, and book festivals.

Book clubs are small reader groups who select, read, and discuss books. Book clubs are often formed around a genre or common interest. You'll find book clubs of every imaginable type in libraries, senior and community centers, faith-based organizations, bookstores, community organizations, retiree living communities and many other

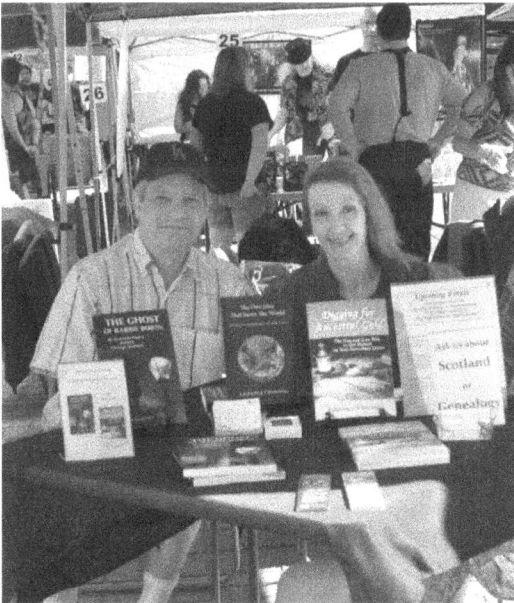

types of gathering places. In many communities, Boomers also can choose from a wide selection of book club Meetups (meetup.com).

Reading Festivals, Events

Bookstores, libraries, and literary organizations sponsor events such as regular readings, discussion groups, and book festivals to bring readers, books, and authors together. Check the websites of your local library, bookstores, or literary or writing groups for information about events and festivals.

The reading and book festivals sponsored in many communities need book-loving volunteers to work in planning, setup, marketing and outreach, and all phases of holding a book festival. In many instances, libraries either sponsor, or partner with festival sponsors such as literary organizations.

Retiree Writers, Authors

If writing is a bucket list item for you, there's no better time to realize your dream. Whether you are as aspiring author, poet, screenwriter, blogger, or playwright, you'll find resources to start you on your writing journey.

No matter where your writing interest is aimed, there are energetic organizations to help you learn, write, get feedback, publish, and socialize.

A wide assortment of writing organizations and Meetups throughout the country offer more choices for authors, writers, bloggers, and poets of all interests and abilities.

Places where all levels of writers and authors can practice and learn their craft include writing groups, community colleges, parks and recreation programs, cultural centers, Meetup groups, and community centers. You'll find writing classes in many genres including fiction, non-fiction, memoir, poetry, short story, screenwriting, business and technical writing, and many others.

CHAPTER 19: MUSEUMS, HISTORY

Is history your passion? Do you love digging into the facts and stories of your community's, state's, or county's past? Or could you take your passion deeper – dig into helping others learn and appreciate history.

Maybe there is a particular facet of history that has captured your fascination – art, architecture, military, politics, transportation, or home life, for example.

Depending on your location, museum exhibits may focus on art, film, architecture, photography, nature, maritime, industry, science, forests and habitat, transportation, cultural museums, private collections, and far more.

History museums in communities throughout the country specialize in exhibits containing artifacts and stories of the state, city, and local communities and neighborhoods. Many museums offer regular events, programs, and tours to enhance the experience for their patrons. Many programs are presented on-line.

Other types of museums focus on more unusual, and often personal, collections such as puppets, hats, games, toys, rocks, and minerals. The list is endless!

Volunteering

Volunteers are the heart of most museums, large or small. Museums and historical sites offer a diverse assortment of roles to fit a volunteer's interests, time, skills, and experience. Whether you want to work with the public or in a behind-the-scenes role, there is something for you.

A great way to share your passion for history is by being a docent or speaker. As a docent – defined as anyone associated with volunteer educational services to a museum – you connect visitors to what they see, conducting tours or talking with groups.

If you are handy with and enjoy working with tools or machinery, museums can use your skills to build and take down exhibits, set up or drive machinery and equipment, or maintain interactive displays. Modelers help build miniature versions of displays. Museums often need assistant archivists who work museum collections to categorize, clean, and store artifacts. Volunteers also may help research or transcribe oral histories.

Volunteers always are needed to greet the public, work in museum stores, help with events and tours, and perform office and fundraising tasks. Writers and editors, graphic artists, designers, and website designers support museum outreach, fundraising and marketing activities. They also serve on advisory and planning committees.

Smaller museums are especially appreciative of volunteers who may take on multiple volunteering roles depending on the museum's needs.

Museum and historical site volunteers receive tremendous personal satisfaction through discovering, preserving, and sharing history. Many museums offer volunteer benefits such as memberships, discounts in museum stores, admission to special events, and recognition through group and individual events.

More Ways to Express Your History Passion

In addition to museums and historical sites, there are many other ways to express your love of history. And have a lot of fun doing it.

Many city celebrations are based on some aspect of its history or the history of a community's unique features, or something for which it is uniquely known. Examples of festival themes may be transportation, parks, unique crops, products, people, and cultures. These celebrations and festivals and celebrations help build a sense of community pride.

Look for opportunities to help these celebrations come alive. Sponsoring organizations such as cities, chambers of commerce, or

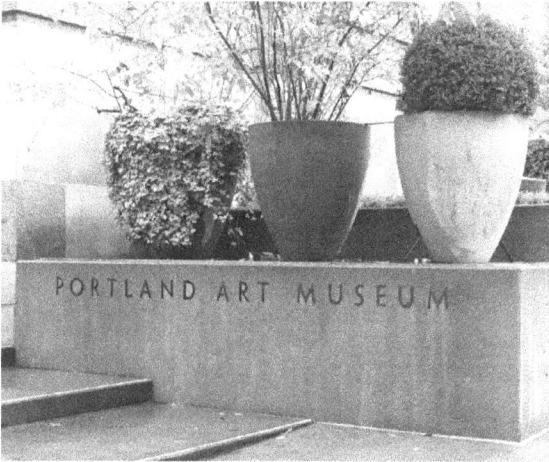

historical societies need volunteer help in organizing, planning, and attending to hundreds of tasks needed for a successful event.

You can even combine interests with theatrics through reenactments of an historical period or event. With an eye on being authentic and true to a time-period or event, some of the most common are military encampments and battles, home and rural life, and lots more.

If your interest lies in a special aspect of history, consider teaching or speaking about it. Look into giving talks in local museums, libraries, and community colleges. Ask around and you'll also find interest in your talk and knowledge at community and senior centers, retiree groups, and community service groups. See *CHAPTER 24: TEACHING, SPEAKING* on page 111 for more ideas!

If you enjoy writing about history, know that many large and small history museums could use your talent to document historical events or periods. You could also create interesting tidbits to publish in newsletters, blogs, and articles.

CHAPTER 20: MUSIC

Does your love of music play some role in your leisure time choices?

Listen around, musical offerings are wonderfully diverse – bluegrass, folk, Indie rock, jazz, classical, pop, or some combination and more.

The music scene offers a tremendous variety of ways to be involved, whether you sing, play an instrument, want to help young musicians learn, or just appreciate listening to music.

Many Boomers broaden their enjoyment of music by volunteering with organizations that perform, teach, and reach out to the music-loving community. Most communities offer opportunities for volunteer choral and instrumental musicians.

Some ways Boomers express their love of music include:

- Performing in community choirs, bands, or orchestras.
- Taking your music to hospitals, nursing homes, and senior facilities.
- Attending live concerts.
- Teaching music.
- Working at concerts behind the scenes.
- Learning or expanding your own music knowledge and skills.

Performing in Local Bands, Orchestras, or Coral Groups

It's not unusual to spot grey-haired and bearded Boomers performing both paid and volunteer gigs at farmers markets, fundraisers, community festivals, and other gathering places. Retiree musicians form small combos and garage bands to further their skills for the plain enjoyment of jamming with others.

Boomers also sing their way through retirement by joining choral groups in their communities and faith organizations, or entertaining at care facilities, retirement communities, and various music venues.

Informal music sessions often gel and evolve into groups that write and perform their own music or perform old familiar music to appreciative Boomers and audiences of all ages.

You'll also find places to share your musical skills in all types of retirement communities, library programs, summer festivals, nonprofit fundraisers, and informal, impromptu get-togethers in a park or neighborhood.

Performing at Hospitals, Care Facilities

Many take their music to people who are recovering or reside in facilities such as hospitals, nursing homes, assisted living centers, senior living communities, and hospice facilities. Musicians perform individually or as a group to brighten the days of people with health and other challenges.

Other places likely to welcome and appreciate your music include senior and community centers, libraries, and parks and recreation programs. Visit their websites or contact the person who coordinates recreation programs.

Teaching Music

If you love teaching, consider helping others learn either as a paid or volunteer instructor. You'll find eager students of all ages – ready for sign up for private lessons or classes through music stores, community colleges, community centers, and parks and recreation programs.

Or consider doing behind the scenes work for nonprofits that help youth learn music. Youth music organizations rely on volunteers to help make music accessible to everyone. Volunteers help teach and mentor, maintain instruments, set up and host events, and help with fundraising and office activities. These nonprofits may require background checks.

Other places to teach music include senior activity centers, senior and retiree living communities, libraries, and parks and recreation programs. Visit their websites or contact the organization directly. For more about places to teach, see *CHAPTER 24: TEACHING, SPEAKING* on page 111.

Do you play an instrument that you'd love to help others learn? What places in your community would welcome your music passion, as well as your skills and time?

Behind the Scenes Volunteers

Concerts in large venues rely on volunteers for a wide variety of roles such as greeting patrons, handing out programs, and ushering. In larger venues, you can join a "Friends-of..." group to fill the volunteer roles. In addition to working directly with performing artists and enjoying your favorite music, volunteer benefits may include concert passes, and patron and recognition events.

Music organizations also need volunteers in tasks such as office data entry and filing, answering the phone, fundraising, marketing, writing, graphic design, ushering, ticket taking, and serving refreshments. Organizations that take music to their audiences may put you to work in outreach programs.

Volunteering information typically is available on an organization's website, or by phone.

Concerts, Festivals

An enjoyable summertime pastime is volunteering at outdoor concerts. Concerts of all types often are sponsored by parks and recreation programs or community business groups all that welcome volunteer help in many roles.

Similarly, if you enjoy being immersed in the music festival scene, volunteer for one! Volunteers work in all aspects of stage set-up and take-down, electronics, assisting performers, serving refreshments and activities unique to the concert. You'll probably land a free ticket, and the opportunity to see your favorite performers up close.

Check out schedules of music festivals and concerts in your area posted on community calendars or by searching on the Internet for music events in your area. Visit websites well in advance to learn about volunteering roles and how to sign up. For more about places to volunteer at festivals and events, see *CHAPTER 10: EVENTS, FESTIVALS* on page 59.

Learning Music

Want to learn to play, practice, or improve your skills on a musical instrument? Check out learning places in your community such as community colleges, parks and recreation programs, and music stores.

Ask local music stores or musicians for other unique starting places, for suggestions or private lessons. If you'd like to practice with others, consider finding jam sessions.

You'll also find lots of online music learning resources including books, live and video training, Facebook and other social media platforms, and online forums. Or search through the YouTube.com site's vast video library for musicians of all experience levels.

CHAPTER 21: SENIOR ASSISTANCE

What types of services are available in your community to help the elderly? Are there ways to get involved and "pay it forward?"

Senior assistance organizations are another way Boomers can give back. "I volunteer for organizations that help seniors because I'll need that help someday," say Boomer volunteers for senior-support organizations. "We provide a little help here and there that allows older adults to age in place."

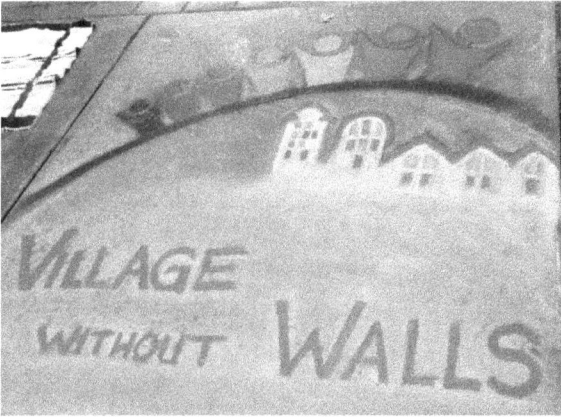

Volunteers pay it forward through nonprofits and other organizations that help seniors in daily living activities such as transportation, in-home assistance, grocery delivery and meals.

Senior-Focused Nonprofits

Examples of senior services organizations in your local community that welcome volunteers are:

- AARP (aarp.org). AARP offers three volunteering programs that provide services to members through its state offices. Tax-Aide volunteers provide free tax-filing help to those who need it most. Driver Safety volunteers help others get on the road to safety as an AARP Driver Safety instructor or coordinator. Volunteers in AARP Experience tutor children in reading.

- AmeriCorps Seniors (nationalservice.gov/programs/senior-corps) is a network of national service programs for Americans 55 years and older. They serve communities in many ways, including tutoring and mentoring students, assisting and caring for the elderly, and supporting relief teams when disasters strike.

- RSVP (createthegood.aarp) is one of the largest volunteer networks in the nation for people over 55. Use the skills and talents you've learned over the years or develop new ones while serving in a variety of community volunteer activities. Search for a program from the website.

- Village to Village Network (vtvnetwork.org). The National Association of the Village Movement is membership-based and brings community Villages together to create a "Village commons." Volunteers provide services to members including transportation, in-home assistance, companionship, gardening advice, phone checks, visits, and as walking partners. Volunteers also help with social events, educational programs, office support, technology assistance, and many other tasks.

- Meals on Wheels. (wheelsamerica.org). A nationwide network of community-based, nonprofit programs dedicated to providing seniors in their communities with the support that enables them to remain living in their own homes. This support is typically a nutritious meal, a friendly visit, and a quick safety check. To sign up, visit the website, or contact the local organization that provides service such as churches, senior centers, and other nonprofits.

- County Programs on Aging. These local agencies ways to provide senior services in your communities. They rely on volunteers in areas such as caregiver support, emergency and disaster shelters, foster grandparent programs, meal sites, senior centers, companion programs, and similar services.

Senior Centers

Other places to help older adults are senior centers that give them a place to hang out, learn new hobbies, get fit, and socialize. Senior centers are important resources for seniors to stay physically and mentally active. Located in most communities, senior centers provide a range of social services to help seniors live, learn, and stay healthy.

Senior centers need volunteers of all ages in a variety of roles including teaching a variety of classes, cooking and serving meals, maintaining libraries, working with technology and computers, playing music, entertaining, and leading trips.

If this interests you, take time to visit your local senior center, or its website, and look into their volunteer openings. Perhaps you could suggest a class or activity that you can organize, or even teach.

CHAPTER 22: SHARING WISDOM

What wisdom and experience could you pass along to other generations?

Boomers who want to pass along the benefits of THE wisdom, knowledge, and expertise they have accumulated over a lifetime have some unique options for giving back.

They volunteer for any of several types of organizations that are specifically built upon the life skills and experience offered by retirees. Skills are sought in areas such as teaching, training, management, accounting, working with youth, and many other areas.

What types of organizations in your area welcome the contributions of older adults to carry out their mission?

In what informal way could you pass the benefits of the wisdom you've acquired over your lifetime?

Options for retirees looking to apply their life experiences are nonprofits that tap into the experience of seniors to carry out their missions. These programs recognize the valuable contributions of older adults who make a difference in our communities. Some examples are:

- AARP Experience Corps. Senior volunteers work with children one-on-one and in groups to help kids in grades K-3 develop literacy skills and build self-confidence. (aarp.org/experience-corps)

- SCORE (Service Corps of Retired Executives). Retired business people provide free business mentoring services to entrepreneurs throughout the county. Volunteers offer specific knowledge based on professional skills or industry, lead seminars and workshops, and expand outreach through alliances in local communities. (score.org)

- AmeriCorps Seniors. A network of national service programs for Americans 55 years and older. They serve communities by tutoring and mentoring students, assisting and caring for the elderly, and supporting relief teams when disasters strike. (nationalservice.gov/programs/senior-corps)

- Encore.org engages older adults in programs that encourage connection and collaboration across generations to address society's greatest problems. Encore.org provides fellowships that match seasoned professionals with social sector organizations.

- National Park Service. Through the NPS VIP program, retirees can volunteer in national parks in exchange for a free RV camping site. NPS posts details and opportunities on their website. (volunteer.gov/s)

Opportunities in Your Community

Some other familiar organizations with local operations that value the experience and skills of seniors include:

- Junior Achievement. A national nonprofit dedicated to educating students in grades K-12 about entrepreneurship, work readiness and financial literacy through experiential, hands-on programs. (juniorachievement.org)

- Habitat for Humanity. Volunteers help build and repair homes and work in the Habitat ReStore retail stores. (habitat.org)

- Boy Scouts and Girl Scouts. Volunteers are leaders and help mentor and help youth learn a variety of skills, many outdoor related. (scouting.org)

- City and County Governments. Many have established retiree volunteer programs for their communities. Nearly all welcome the life experience and wisdom retirees bring on various advisory committees and boards. See *CHAPTER 13: GOVERNMENT SERVICE* on page 77.

What organizations in your community focus on intergenerational projects and activities?

CHAPTER 23: SOCIAL CONNECTIONS

We are hard-wired to be socially active and engaged as a community. Research confirms what experience tells us – positive connections with

family and friends make us healthier and happier and improve everyone's lives. Without connections we become lonely, isolated, and just a touch crabby!

Retirees are no strangers to changes that upend our social lives. Life-changing events such as retirement and loss of daily people contact, make us aware of our need for new social activities. Many view retirement as the time to make new friends as they try out new things! We find connections and community anywhere we gather around a common interest. Surrounding us are literally hundreds of places to meet and connect with others – places of worship, neighborhoods, community centers – in classes and volunteer work, just for starters.

Places for Social Groupies

Most communities in our country offer almost unlimited options for social engagement. In fact, as you browse this book, nearly type of interest and activity points to places where Boomers and retirees meet and connect with people around a common interest such as …

- Community, Adult, Senior Centers. Your local community and senior centers are gathering places specifically designed for social activity. They encourage new and current members to take part in a wide variety of classes, workshops, excursions, and social clubs.

- Community College Programs. Community colleges offer programs and activities on their academic schedules specifically for retired adults and seniors, or of interest to seniors, with emphasis on social learning activities. See *CHAPTER 17: LEARN SOMETHING NEW* on page 91.

- Faith-based Organizations. Retirees benefit in many ways by involvement in faith-based organizations and the giving of their time and energy in causes their organization supports: a sense of connection to something beyond themselves, the connections and benefits of social aspect, and the satisfaction of helping others.

- Hobby Groups. The common interest we find in hobbies naturally connects us. Many hobbies bring us together to work on projects, study more about our pastimes and socialize. *See CHAPTER 16: HOBBIES* on page 89.

- Meetups. These A-Z groups in your area groups formed around a common interest or activity, very social by nature, found at Meetup.com. Meetups run the gamut of interests – from commonplace to unusual and everything in between.

- Outdoor and Fitness Groups. Outdoor groups of all types are common everywhere. You'll find groups that walk, hike, run, play pickleball, swim, golf, garden…you get the idea. Outdoorsy types connect through a passion for their activity and being out in nature, as well as a liking for social gatherings. For information on outdoor and fitness groups, see *CHAPTER 7: CARE FOR THE ENVIRONMENT* on page 51; *CHAPTER 11: FITNESS, HEALTHY LIVING* on page 63; *CHAPTER 12: GARDENING: TEND A GARDEN* on page 73; *CHAPTER 14: HIKING, WALKING* on page 85; *CHAPTER 25: THE GREAT OUTDOORS* on page 117.

- Parks and Recreation Programs. Community parks and recreation programs offer places to connect and socialize with like-minded seniors and adults. These programs include an ever-changing variety of classes and activities. See *CHAPTER 17: LEARN SOMETHING NEW* on page 91.

- Retirement, Senior Living Communities. If you live in a retirement community, you already know that social engagement is a central attraction for many. Communities of retirees offer a wide variety of activities, centered on learning and socializing, and fun!

- Volunteering. Part of our social nature is a desire to make our communities better places to live, work, and play. By volunteering we work side-by-side with others to help others. Learn more about volunteering in *CHAPTER 3: VOLUNTEERING* on page 25.

CHAPTER 24: TEACHING, SPEAKING

How would you finish this sentence?

I would love to use my knowledge of _____
to help people such as _____ *learn about*
_____-
_____.

We each have acquired knowledge about and skills for something. We may have acquired it through school, work, a hobby, or people we hang with. Some came naturally; others we've had to learn. *So, is it now time to share that with others?*

For example, you may know how to create a quilt or knit a hat, build a cedar strip canoe, play the guitar, write a short story or poem, play pinochle, tie a fly, or kayak down a river.

Can you cook a specialty dish? Do you know how to set up a chart of accounts, put up a website, or use spreadsheet software? Maybe you're passionate about some interesting aspect of history, current event or issue, a biography, an artist, or a musician or author.

Think about it – if you're interested, others are too. Someone wants to know what you know. So why not help them learn? Find your own teach-talk-tutor-train niche and go for it! You have more to share than you think.

While we often use teaching, talking (speaking), tutoring, and training interchangeably, there are differences:

- TEACHING – Usually occurs in a formal group classroom setting, where you are the leader of a specific curriculum. A community college course on local history, for example.

- TALKING (SPEAKING) – Primarily from a platform before a group, where you are presenting as a keynote or workshop speaker. A civic, church, or social group speech on healthy aging, for example.

- TUTORING – Happens one-on-one, where you coach and guide another individual to learn from you. Helping students improve their math skills, for example.

- TRAINING – Can be for an individual or group, where you are guiding their learning and mastery of a specific set of skills. Guiding people on how to use a computer software program, for example.

Discover Your Niche

To figure out how best to position yourself, refer back to your self-understanding questions. Think about:

1. What is your passion and knowledge base?
2. Who wants to learn this knowledge?
3. Where can you reach those people and share what you know?

What to Teach?

What are you good at? What do you know a lot about? For what information do people come to you? What have you been invited to give presentations about?

Your past jobs and career are fertile discovery fields. *What did you enjoy most? For what do you have special knowledge and expertise in your field?*

Or do you have experience in a professional organization? For example, a special knowledge of technology, a product or service, current industry trends, or research?

What is your favorite hobby or pastime? Consider turning the hobby you love into your perfect volunteer opportunity. Help inspire others to learn from your expertise. *What about your hobbies or past hobbies? Do you build stuff? Make jewelry? Play cards, sew, knit, quilt, enjoy birding? Do you take photos or build models? Can you help others seek out local adventures? Do you write stories or novels?*

How about activities? What outdoorsy pursuits do you particularly enjoy and know about? Are you a special-interest gardener or a fisherman? Do you cycle, walk, hike, swim, play golf, tennis or pickleball? Would you love to help others learn?

Are there subjects you could tutor others on? For example, helping youth or adults with reading, math, science, writing, learning English, managing finances?

Who are Your Learners?

Next, think about the types of people who need the knowledge and experience you offer.

Are they children, adults, seniors, or some combination? What are their situations? How will you reach them? Are you interested in one-on-one, smaller, or larger groups? Narrow your choices down as much as possible.

Do you want to help people who are struggling with overcoming difficult life situations? Many social service organizations need people who can step in and serve in this important way.

Where to Share?

Where is your best place to teach-talk-tutor-train? Do you need the structure of an educational institution, library, or sponsor group? What learning situations would you prefer? Some may require formal education and credentials, others emphasize experience.

A multitude of teaching opportunities are found in and beyond traditional learning places – schools, universities, and community colleges. Many Boomers share their expertise in the less formal community education programs.

The following types of organizations may offer says to share your knowledge and expertise. To find them, start by visiting the organization's website, viewing a course catalog, visiting the volunteer web page, or contacting the organization directly by phone or email. Ask for the appropriate contact person.

- Adult and Senior Enrichment Programs. Often sponsored by local colleges and universities, these programs offer seniors a wide variety of classes ranging from health and fitness, current events, local history, contemporary world problems, and many other topics of interest. Many feature talks by local speakers and authors.

- Community and Senior Centers. Located in communities throughout the country, senior centers provide a range of social services, classes, and workshops to help seniors live, learn, thrive, and socialize. Many offer programs and speakers on a wide variety of topics such as various history and current events topics, health education programs and activities. Suggest an activity or class you could offer on your specialty, favorite pastime, or interest.

- Community Business and Service Organizations. Depending on your area of expertise, all types of community organizations seek speakers on topics of interest to their members. Their programs vary from current events to interesting aspects of community businesses, organizations, history, and development.

- Community Service Tutoring. Many schools and nonprofits seek tutors to help children and adults with reading, art, photography, music, sports, daily living skills, and social services. See postings on an organization's volunteer page.

- Libraries and Museums. Libraries invite speakers to share their knowledge, skills, and expertise on a wide variety of topics. Library programs include author talks, art shows, cultural festivals, lectures, and abundant hands-on learning opportunities. Libraries also offer how-to programs on all varieties of hobbies, arts and crafts, and writing and publishing, and much more.

Local museums and historical societies may offer teaching and speaking opportunities, especially for history buffs. Most museums offer programs to enrich understanding of the history behind their collections. And welcome local experts!

• Medical Centers. Another place to check out are healthcare organizations that offer health-related classes to patients and members, and to the community at large. Some have online classes and videos. See the types of classes offered on their websites and contact the person in charge of community education.

• Online Teaching. For a variety of reasons, more learning organizations offer a growing number and types of online classes. The flipside of online learning is online teaching. Consider turning your teaching or speaking expertise into an online class or talk. Start with local colleges, community centers and other learning venues. A digital recording of yourself teaching or speaking is also helpful when presenting your class as an option.

• Parks and Rec Programs. Parks programs offer activities for all ages. In addition to outdoor activities, many also offer indoor recreation programs such as music, dancing, healthy living, hobbies, and more. Those interested in teaching should view the organization's activity catalog and contact the person in charge of classes.

• Schools, Universities and Colleges. In addition to credit and non-credit community education classes, many colleges offer other programs and activities that provide volunteer (and paid!) speaking opportunities. Look for contact information or applications in course catalogs. Interested speakers may also contact the college directly. Many schools and nonprofits also seek tutors to help children with reading, art, music, and sports, as well as social skills.

CHAPTER 25: THE GREAT OUTDOORS

Maybe you've spent years chained to a desk, your eyes radar-locked on a computer spreadsheet and now, on the cusp of your next phase, it's time for a change of scenery!

You can morph from corporate beige to green without a digital device. Experience tangible, touchable scenery. Photograph worthy landmarks. Go outside, away from all things electronic. Surround yourself with forests, nature parks, lakes, and rivers. Backdrop your tableau with blue, or grey sky – even the rain and snow have great beauty. Photograph blooming cactus, wander through gently swaying palm trees or collect shells along white sandy beaches. Go to places where you can infuse fresh air into a foggy brain.

Ours is a county of rocky terraine, gentle coastlines, snow capped mountains, deserts, mountain trails, rivers, lakes, and out-of-the-way wetlands, watersheds, and natural dramatic features beckoning to be explored. Our large and small city towns display their own individual architectural interest, commercial uniqueness, and walkability.

Discover the abundant neighborhood parks right in your backyard. And don't forget your own community's unique features and hidden nature gems within walking and driving distance.

Take it Outside!

In your next phase plan, then, turn electronics to "Not Now" mode, think about what appeals to you, and take yourself outside! Look for:

- Fitness Sports and Activities. Find places to enjoy walking, running, cycling, skiing, jogging, swimming, pickleball, kayaking, and more. See more about outdoor health and fitness options *in CHAPTER 11: FITNESS*, HEALTHY LIVING on page 63.

- Gardening. Get the dirt on local gardening and gardens; how to enjoy, learn, socialize, and grow stuff in a garden. See *CHAPTER 12: GARDENING* on page 73.

- Hiking and Walking. Choose from unlimited places to hike and walk in neighborhoods, in forests, parks, and cities, around outdoor art venues, on mountain trails, and unique local places. See *CHAPTER 15: HIKING, WALKING* on page 85.

  • Local Adventures. Day trip to new outdoor experiences and adventures. Seek out rivers, lakes, small towns, parks, and nature centers. Check your local Chamber of Commerce or Tourism organizations. For ideas to get you started, see *CHAPTER 27: TRAVEL* on page 123.

- Outdoor Concerts, Farmers Markets, Art Shows. What better way to blend culture and outdoors in a spring, summer or fall festival? Look for those centered around art, music, food, ethnic traditions, history, city celebrations, and more. See *CHAPTER 10: EVENTS, FESTIVALS* on page 59.

- Outdoor Volunteering. Volunteer at parks, natural areas, wildlife refuges, trails, rivers, gardens, and many other places. See *CHAPTER 7: CARE FOR THE ENVIRONMENT* on page 51, and *CHAPTER 12: GARDENING* on page 73.

CHAPTER 26: THEATER, PERFORMANCE

Are you among the many Boomers who love live theater and performances and want to help enrich the theater experience in some way?

Do you secretly yearn to get on stage? Or volunteer behind the scenes? What resonates with you? Where can you get involved?

The Theater Scene

If you've secretly (or openly) wanted to be involved in theater, an ever-changing performance scene offers limitless opportunities to engage in all aspects of theater.

Many cities and communities beckon theater-lovers with rich, vibrant, opportunities for a broad range of interests. Large, established venues anchor the theatrical panorama, enriched with a delightful, diverse mixture of quality regional and local productions.

Depending on your area, your choices may range from innovative and experimental, to ethnic and social statement, ambitious blends with original music and visual arts media, and delightful homegrown productions.

Get on Stage: Acting and Storytelling

Want to lose the timid and get on stage? Haven't acted since junior high?

You're in the right place. Do a little homework first, though, because theaters have different needs and prerequisites for performers. Large and medium-sized professional theaters generally cast and hire equity and non-equity actors. Smaller and independent theaters may stage productions with a volunteer cast. Some train you in advance. Others give you on-the-set training.

Smaller community theaters are good starting places because of their all-volunteer cast and crew. In many community theaters, you can audition to act, understudy someone, or work hands-on behind the scenes. Tasks such as building and taking down sets, changing scenes, sewing costumes, running lights, and helping on show nights is a fun way to learn theater ins and outs.

Do you have a favorite story or two you'd like to share on stage?

Storytelling is another great way to get in front of an audience. Storytellers share vivid personal stories on stage, believing that to be human is to have a story to share. Special workshops sponsored by libraries, community colleges, and other groups, help storytellers learn how to develop and present stories to live audiences.

Behind the Scenes

Did you ever realize that performance by actors, directors, and other performers is simply the tip of the iceberg of the live stage?

Off-stage roles are filled with people like you who make the show go on. Volunteers enjoy being creatively involved in making plays happen

and using a special skill or interest such as technology, construction, costuming, music, sound and lighting set up, organizing, or meeting the public. All of these roles support the simple desire to experience it up close.

Volunteers greet and usher. They design, build, and change sets, sew costumes, apply makeup. They manage

lighting, sound, and music. Many work in the back office selling tickets, creating flyers, maintaining lists, and doing mailings. Others create brochures and take photos. You might like to sell refreshments and gifts, meet the public at special events and outreach activities, or plan those activities.

Major Theaters

If you volunteer through a major theater, you'll join a well-established volunteer organization that may have hundreds of volunteers (lots of retirees), who donate hours as ushers, greeters, gift shop attendees, tour guides, reception desk attendants, office assistants, and receptionists.

Medium-Size and Regional Theater

Medium-size professional and non-professional companies perform in area downtowns and suburbs. Volunteers usher, sell concessions and merchandise, help patrons, do hands-on behind-the-scenes tasks, sew costumes, build sets, and work in outreach.

Local and Independent Theater

Smaller independent and home-grown performing groups are often scattered throughout a community. Theater groups entertain in theaters, converted buildings, churches, and warehouses. Many are all-volunteer – from actors and directors to many behind-the-scenes stage production, office, and administrative roles.

Dance

Dance-loving volunteers can also participate in performing arts. Performances in many cities range from ballet concerts to contemporary work by local companies and collaborations with other art forms. Many take their innovations to local communities. Volunteers perform various behind the scenes roles as they do in other performance genres.

Performing Arts Festivals

Volunteering in a wide variety of roles at annual theater festivals is another way to experience traditional as well new, emerging fringe theater, dance, and other performances.

As in many types of festivals, volunteers are needed to plan, line up facilities, work with performers and promoters, get the word out, and attend to thousands of behind-the-scenes details.

For more on festival volunteering, see *CHAPTER 10: EVENTS, FESTIVALS* on page 59.

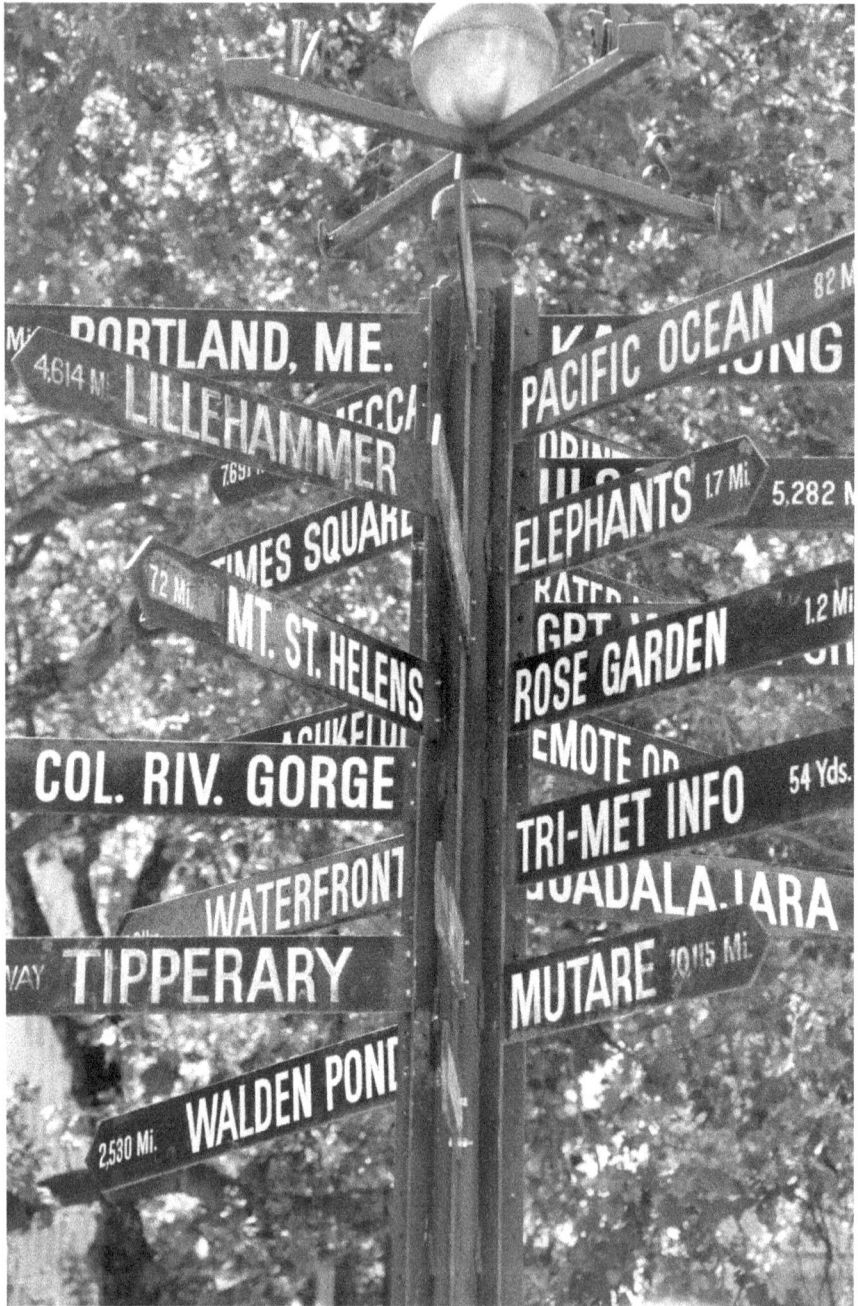

CHAPTER 27: TRAVEL

While travel to "…someplace I've always wanted to visit…" is on many Boomer bucket lists, there are many more ways to create meaningful experiences through local, regional, national, or international travel.

Start by thinking about your passions and interests, and the types of experiences you enjoy. Then look at the ways travel could enhance or enrich those. For example, if you enjoy cooking, you could enroll in classes in the country of your favorite food, take classes on a cruise, or enjoy either of these with your cooking group.

Another popular option are intergenerational trips, sharing a travel passion with kids, grandkids, grandparents, or others. For example:

- Heritage trips. Find places to research the history of your ancestors or study the history of an area of interest.

- Milestone trips. Celebrate a special occasion such as a birthday, anniversary, or retirement (Ta-Da!), to create a lasting memory.

- Hobby or interest. You have as many unlimited options as there are hobbies. Take classes, or just enjoy your hobby in other states or countries. Learn woodworking, art, music, sailing, hiking, culinary arts, or more about your favorite varietals.

- Sports and outdoors. Grab your clubs and rackets and skates, hiking boots, boards and skis, and whatever else you need to get up, get out, and take on your sport or activity at a new destination!

Good starting points to research travel are travel classes and group excursions offered by many community colleges and other organizations in local communities.

RV Travel

Another very popular bucket list option for millions of retirees is hitting the road by RV (recreational vehicle). Millions of RVers across the country express their wanderlust by either driving or pulling their shelter to thousands of get-away destinations near and far.

Weekend, months, or seasonal trips. They're off to leave behind yardwork and chores, experiences new places, and enjoy new and old friends, and companions. With groups or solo to remote areas.

If you're thinking that RVing may be for you, do your research. Consider ways to try out the lifestyle and responsibilities and costs before taking the plunge. Ease into RVing by visiting any number of online forums, discussion groups, and talk with people you know.

Local Adventures: Day Tripping

How often do we say, "I only visit local sights when guests come to town!" Well, it may be time to venture out as a tourist in your own town. You'll likely find no better day-tripping paradise than driving to

destinations in your own local and regional communities. You may be delightfully surprised with new discoveries for everyone. Day trip solo, with friends, or find a group.

In many areas, you needn't travel far to enjoy a forest, wetlands, shipyard, river city, valley, beautiful garden, outdoor art collection, seasonal farmers market, art fair, history museum, local oddity, and on and on.

Day trip to big, medium, small, and micro-towns. Dig out the history and museums. Discover where communities blend new urban with refurbished old and real old, still original, and somewhere in between.

While many places only can be reached by car, others may be near to public light-rail-streetcar-bus systems, or ferry systems. Venturing out, you'll find more than just big trees growing taller. You'll find that just a little research – in your libraries, the local sections of bookstores, Chamber of Commerce offices, and visitor's centers – will bring you pleasant surprises as you explore your own back yard.

Places to Start

Here are some ideas to whet your local journey appetite and the tip of the iceberg when it comes to exploring your own town:

- Pick a cultural destination from your area's collection of art galleries, museums, historical sites, and other cultural centers.

- Enjoy the unique character, history, and ambiance of nearby small towns and communities. Walk about and visit local shops, bakeries, eateries, coffee shops, and points of interest. Take several trips to appreciate their unique character and hidden nooks and crannies.

- Visit city, chamber of commerce or visitor center websites for maps, lists of attractions and walking tour maps of historical or natural interest.

- Get near water. Enjoy scenic river walks or boat excursions. take a checklist tour of bridges and to spot natural features.

- Tour campuses of older colleges and universities, especially for wonderful surprises of art, architecture, sculpture, and landscaping, especially old heritage buildings and trees. Look for good strolling campuses in neighboring communities.

- Take self-guided walking tours of area communities using free maps and descriptions available historical groups and tourism information stops. Look into routes mapped out by your local Volkssport organizations that meander through downtowns, neighborhoods, historical areas, parks, and other points of interest.

- Put free and inexpensive local festivals and events on your watch list. For more ideas, check community calendars on the websites of Chamber of Commerce, cities, counties, and tourism organizations.

- Drive through the countryside and visit produce and flower farms, and take in hot apple cider and glazed donuts, enjoy seasonal ripening of pumpkins, fruits and vegetables, and flowers.

Group Day Trips

If group day outings appeal to you, look into organizations that offer group outings and trips such as community colleges, parks programs, retirement communities, and community centers. You'll likely find inexpensive, convenient ways to visit local and regional attractions, natural landscapes, and diverse off-the-beaten-path destinations.

Travel Abroad

Many retirees find the lure of international travel irresistible and set out to learn about and experience different cultures up close. Today's interconnected world brings abundant resources and information right to our electronic devices. Connect to vast libraries of travel information, on-line blogs and chats, podcasts, newsletters, classes and much more.

ABOUT THE AUTHOR

Janet Farr (Jan) is a self-proclaimed authentic Boomer on the loose. Typical of Baby Boomers beyond that "certain age," Jan is re-inventing a 40+ year career experience as a business and technical writer. She also shares that boomer-typical desire to pursue meaning in her next phase in ways that make a positive difference in the lives of others.

Jan is the author of *Boomers on the Loose®* in Portland, publishing the second edition in 2020. Enhancing what she learned about the abundance retiree interests, aspirations, and options everywhere, she created *Boomers on the Loose®* to share this knowledge with a wider, national audience.

Jan is a transplant from the Kansas City area, and before that, central Michigan. In 2009 she finally took steps to realize her dream to experience the unique Pacific Northwest outdoor lifestyle, and took off for Portland, Oregon. She currently resides in Olympia, Washington.

She loves exploring northwest forests, wetlands, mountains, gardens, the coast, wine country, cities, towns, and villages, large and small. And she especially enjoys experiencing the homegrown arts, music, and culture scene – thriving side-by-side with the high-profile – the caring-for-people attitude, the amazing summers and yes, even the rain making the elegant ruggedness possible.

Not to mention, lots of amateur photo opportunities.

She's cursed with an eagerness to research and organize vast amounts of information into useful chunks that delight, surprise, and help her Boomer retiree audience find meaning in their own lives.

INDEX

www.ingramcontent.com/pod-product-compliance
Lightning Source LLC
Chambersburg PA
CBHW050733030426
42336CB00012B/1538